REFORMING REGULATION

ROGER G. NOLL

REFORMING REGULATION
An Evaluation of the Ash Council Proposals

A Staff Paper

Studies in the Regulation of Economic Activity
THE BROOKINGS INSTITUTION
Washington, D.C.

THE BROOKINGS INSTITUTION is an independent organization devoted to nonpartisan research, education, and publication in economics, government, foreign policy, and the social sciences generally. Its principal purposes are to aid in the development of sound public policies and to promote public understanding of issues of national importance.

The Institution was founded on December 8, 1927, to merge the activities of the Institute for Government Research, founded in 1916, the Institute of Economics, founded in 1922, and the Robert Brookings Graduate School of Economics and Government, founded in 1924.

The general administration of the Institution is the responsibility of a Board of Trustees charged with maintaining the independence of the staff and fostering the most favorable conditions for creative research and education. The immediate direction of the policies, program, and staff of the Institution is vested in the President, assisted by an advisory committee of the officers and staff.

In publishing a study, the Institution presents it as a competent treatment of a subject worthy of public consideration. The interpretations and conclusions in such publications are those of the author or authors and do not necessarily reflect the views of the other staff members, officers, or trustees of the Brookings Institution.

FOREWORD

On February 11, 1971, President Nixon released the report on the independent regulatory agencies of his Advisory Council on Executive Organization (called the Ash Council after its chairman, Roy L. Ash). The President expressed hope that the report would "stimulate a vigorous public discussion" and called on "the broadest possible range of groups and individuals concerned and affected ... to respond with their comments and criticisms." As the President said, the regulatory agencies were created "to protect the members of the consuming public against market abuses over which they had little or no control." The object of both the Ash Council report and of this evaluation is to assist in the public search for reforms that serve this end.

The literature of law, economics, and political science offers many important insights into the process and effects of regulation. This paper seeks to summarize some of those ideas in a way that will facilitate public discussion of the Ash Council proposals and of the performance of the regulatory agencies. It is not meant as an original piece of scholarly research, but as a synthesis of the work of scholars from several disciplines.

The Ash Council report suggests that a principal cause of regulatory failure and inefficiency lies in the organization of regulation. The report is critical of the independent, collegial body as a vehicle for formulating and implementing regulatory policy. This paper presents an alternative view—that the regulatory process is inherently flawed, regardless of the form of organization of the regulatory agencies. Both the laws establishing regulatory mandates and the political environment in which regulation operates are suggested as possible causes of regulatory weakness.

Several individual regulatory agencies are examined by the principal author with the collaboration of others whose names appear in the table of contents. Among the agencies examined are a number not discussed in the Ash Council report that are organized along the lines proposed by the Council—headed by a single administrator and lodged in the executive branch. These discussions lead the author to conclude that nearly all regulatory authorities, however structured and wherever lodged, are subject to generally similar criticisms: that their procedures are cumbersome, that they do not make their policies sufficiently clear, and that they tend to be overly responsive to the interests of the industries they regulate.

The final chapter summarizes the views of a number of experts who met at the Brookings Institution to discuss the Ash Council report and an earlier version of this manuscript. Their names are given in Appendix B. Among many other persons who contributed valuable comments and advice, the author wishes especially to thank Roger C. Cramton, Richard M. Cyert, John A. Ferejohn, Edwin T. Haefele, William K. Jones, James W. McKie, and Merton J. Peck. He would also like to thank Susan Nelson for research assistance, Evelyn Fisher for checking citations and facts, and Elizabeth Keyser and Gail Shaefer for secretarial support.

This staff paper is part of the Brookings program of Studies in the Regulation of Economic Activity, designed to promote scholarly work on issues of public concern in the field of economic regulation. Supported by a grant from the Ford Foundation, this research is part of the Brookings Economic Studies Program directed by Joseph A. Pechman. Assisting Mr. Pechman in the direction of Studies in the Regulation of Economic Activity is the author of this staff paper, Roger Noll, a senior fellow at Brookings. The views expressed are those of the author; they should not be ascribed to the trustees, officers, or other staff members of the Brookings Institution or of the Ford Foundation.

KERMIT GORDON
President

August 1971
Washington, D.C.

CONTENTS

CHAPTER ONE

INTRODUCTION

For thirty-five years, numerous reports by businessmen, lawyers, political scientists, economists, and consumer advocates have agreed that government regulation of business is in dire need of reform.

The latest in a long series of pleas for fundamental changes in regulation was submitted to the White House on January 30, 1971, by the President's Advisory Council on Executive Organization. This group—known as the Ash Council for its chairman, Roy L. Ash—was asked by the President to study the independent regulatory agencies of the federal government and recommend organizational improvements.[1] This paper analyzes the Council's proposals within a broad framework of regulatory problems.

Previous reform proposals have centered around three fundamental issues: (1) Administrative procedures—how should the methods used by agencies in gathering information and making decisions be set up in order to guard against arbitrary and unfair decisions? (2) The scope of regulation—what private economic decisions ought to be subject to governmental review and control, and what performance objectives should regulation be striving for? And (3) the effectiveness of regulation—how can regulatory authorities be made to do a better job in terms of both making good choices as to which specific private decisions to regulate and achieving the objective of protecting the public interest?

1. In addition to Mr. Ash, President of Litton Industries, Inc., the Council members were George P. Baker, former Dean of the Harvard University Graduate School of Business Administration; John B. Connally, former Governor of Texas and now Secretary of the Treasury; Frederick R. Kappel, former Chairman of the Board of the American Telephone & Telegraph Company; and Walter N. Thayer, President of Whitney Communications Corporation. The Council's findings are entitled *A New Regulatory Framework: Report on Selected Independent Regulatory Agencies* (Government Printing Office, 1971). Among the other administrative matters studied by the Council were the organization of the Executive Office of the President and the functional organization and size of the Cabinet. The new Environmental Protection Agency, the reorganization of the Bureau of the Budget into the Office of Management and Budget, and the Domestic Affairs Council were all initially proposed in other reports by the Ash Council.

In the first arena, the battle has been largely—perhaps excessively—won. The 1946 Administrative Procedure Act, the result of a decade of pressure from the legal fraternity, established elaborate formal rules of behavior for regulatory agencies. The law provides the parties to regulatory cases and the courts with ample ammunition to use if regulatory agencies behave cavalierly in investigating and deciding regulatory issues—for instance, by failing to keep a record, adopting discriminatory rules of standing, improperly assigning the burden of proof, and so on.

If any major battle for reform of administrative procedures remains to be fought, it is probably for some relaxation of the present strictures. The elaborate procedures established for and by regulatory agencies run the risk of focusing excessive attention on legal formalities, at the expense of the substantive economic and social issues of regulation. In many cases the only real threat to a decision by an agency is an appeal to the courts on grounds of improper agency procedure; thus the agency has a strong incentive to make certain of its procedural position.

The second and third points of controversy remain virtually unchanged after three decades of debate. The Ash Council's recommendations deal only with the effectiveness question. Their characterization of the barriers to effective regulation and their proposals for reform are not new (nor are they so represented). What the Council has done is to weave into a somewhat new fabric a number of threads of criticism and recommendations that have reappeared periodically since the 1930s. They thus have served the functions of keeping the issue of the structure of regulation in the public conscience and reminding government and the public once again of the virtually unanimous opinion of informed observers that reform of regulation is necessary. In this the Council has performed a useful service.

Yet in considering only organizational issues, the Council report perhaps understates the seriousness and complexity of the failures of regulation. It describes in only a cursory manner the nature of the problems of regulation, the possible causes of these problems, and the alternative solutions. This paper seeks to advance the discussion of regulatory reform by raising a number of issues either overlooked or mentioned only briefly by the Council. The problems of regulation run much deeper than the Ash report implies, perhaps reaching to the heart of the democratic process itself. This analysis attempts to bring together several current, somewhat mutually inconsistent, lines of thought on the problems of regulation, raising important issues that need to be dealt with in formulating a new scope and structure of government controls over business behavior.

Chapter 2 summarizes the main points made by the Ash Council and presents a brief evaluation of the report. Chapter 3 discusses the failings of regulation in somewhat greater detail than does the report, examining several manifestations of the excessive sensitivity of regulatory agencies to the welfare of the industries they regulate. The Ash report's explanation of this behavior might be characterized as the error-by-incompetence view, as opposed to the error-by-design view found in much of the professional literature on regulation.

Chapter 4 deals with legal-political theories of regulation. It seeks to present some plausible generalities about the regulatory process that can serve to explain why agencies behave as they do and that can predict how changes in the organization, position in the governmental structure, and legislative mandate of agencies might alter their behavior. Chapter 5 broadens the scope of the discussion to several agencies not examined in the Ash report. Extending the domain of analysis serves two purposes. First, it provides information about the pervasiveness of the problems identified by the Ash Council. Second, since the structure of some agencies is similar to the new organization of the independent agencies proposed by the Council, it presents an opportunity to test whether the Ash Council recommendations could improve the effectiveness of regulation. Chapter 6 discusses the problems of legalism, staffing, and agency resource allocation, and how they relate to the Ash proposals. Chapter 7 offers some alternatives to the Council's reform proposals. Chapter 8 summarizes the Brookings conference on regulatory reform, for which the other chapters served as a background paper.

The observations and analyses are, by intention, controversial. The object of this paper is to crystallize the issues that are relevant to making new public policy in the area of business regulation. It does not contain new information on the effects of regulation; rather it summarizes an immense body of opinion on these issues in a way that is intended to facilitate fruitful debate.

CHAPTER TWO

A SUMMARY OF THE ASH COUNCIL REPORT

According to the Ash report, the independent regulatory agencies have proven insufficiently flexible and adaptable in dealing with the continuing changes in the industries they regulate and in the U.S. economy generally. To carry out their mandate to regulate in the public interest, the regulatory agencies must be capable of sensing and responding with dispatch to the changing economic, technological, and social scene. But, according to the Council, the agencies have been too rigid to respond to changes in the regulatory environment and consequently have failed, presumably by an increasingly wide margin, to act in the public interest.

The Ash Council report does not really attempt to defend this proposition; only in the case of transportation regulation does the Council try to illustrate the problems arising from rigidity in the regulatory agencies. The report describes several ways in which the organizational structure of regulation encourages rigidity and proposes changes that would lead to more effective regulation.[1] While the report mixes the recitation of problems in regulation with the proposed changes in structure, in the following pages these two general issues are separated.

The Diagnosis: Why Are Regulatory Agencies Inflexible?

The Ash Council believes that the performance of regulatory agencies has been unsatisfactory because of the organization of regulation: the place of the agencies in the governmental establishment and the structure of the agencies themselves. The principal alternative views (discussed at length in later chapters) are that the laws establishing and governing regulatory agencies are

1. The Council's own summary of its findings and recommendations is included as Appendix A of this paper.

4

inadequate, and that effective regulation is not possible in a large, pluralistic representative democracy.

The regulatory agencies, as described by the Council, all have the following characteristics.

1. In charge of the agency is a tribunal of essentially co-equal commissioners, responsible for establishing agency policies, making final decisions in specific cases coming before the agency, and managing the activities of the staff (although in some agencies the last responsibility is largely the domain of the chairman of the commission).

2. The agency is formally independent of the other three branches of government in that only an act of Congress, not vetoed by the President and not declared invalid by the courts, can, in principle at least, force an agency to change a policy or reverse a decision as long as the agency operates within the delegation of power legislated by the Congress and obeys certain procedural rules.

3. The legislation defining the mandate of the agency is general and vague, typically giving the agency the responsibility and the power to regulate a particular industry, activity, or resource in the public interest; sometimes the legislation lists some considerations the agency must take into account in making decisions, but these considerations are normally general, all encompassing, and mutually inconsistent, and in reality constrain the decision-making power of the agency very little.

4. The methods of collecting information and reaching decisions practiced by the agencies, now formally codified in legislation, are similar to the practices of the federal courts; the commission resembles a court in its behavior in that it tends to focus on individual cases rather than the broad policy issues that underlie them, typically hearing the pleadings of parties to a dispute and reaching a decision based on the formal record built through the advocacy proceedings.

The Ash Council cites several consequences of these characteristics that it believes to be the source of rigidity in the agencies.

Lack of Accountability

In building an institution largely independent of the President, the Congress has, according to the Council, made regulation independent of congressional influence as well. As a result, the agencies are shielded from public opinion and the structural changes occurring in society. Public policy toward the national economy, as reflected in legislation by the Congress and executive action by the administration, is constantly changing in response to the demands of society as expressed through the political process. These changes in policy are to some extent a response to the continuing change in the economic and social structure of the nation. By insulating the regulatory agencies from the political system, the Congress has constructed a major impediment to adaptability within the agencies, for the political system has no means of translating society's demands for change into regulatory policy. Furthermore, because the agencies are independent of each other, their policies are uncoordinated, despite the obvious interrelationships among many of the regulated industries. Finally, the independence of the agencies causes them to have no political champion. As a result, they have great difficulty getting Congress to provide adequate budgets and new or amended legislation.

The Collegial Form

A commission of co-equal members is said to be inherently ineffective for several reasons.

1. A collegial body has difficulty making general policy and rules, since minor differences of opinion among the members—that may lead to different conclusions in only a small fraction of individual cases—can make agreement on all-encompassing decisions difficult to reach. Consequently collegial bodies have a tendency to take the case-by-case approach to decision making, squandering their time in adjudicating a large number of similar cases and agonizing anew and at length every case that depends upon a particularly difficult general policy issue. The long delays in dealing with each case lead to large backloads of undecided cases. Moreover, all policies, developing as they do from case precedents, are after-the-fact rather than anticipatory.

2. Collegial bodies are not efficient managers of a bureaucracy. Staff members have divided loyalties, even if one commissioner is technically responsible for directing them. Furthermore, agency resources are likely to be organized around the information flows required by a case-by-case approach, leaving few staff members free to analyze the regulated industry, the general effectiveness of regulation, and the public interest in regulatory policy.

3. Coordination among regulatory agencies and between an agency and the other branches of government, made difficult by independence, is made impossible by the collegial form. Coordination must involve at least a majority of each commission. The inability of the members of a commission to agree on general policy prevents each agency from negotiating from specific policy grounds. Communication between agencies must consequently involve specific cases; therefore, truly effective coordination would require an increase of several fold in the number of cases considered by each commissioner and an

unworkably large number of individuals searching for common grounds for agreement on each issue.

4. The problem of finding a majority position on each case places a premium on procedural solutions. If a decision can be reached solely on the grounds of whether all the parties to an issue followed all of the procedural rules in presenting their cases, the necessity for finding common policy viewpoints is eliminated. Consequently, collegial bodies tend to develop complicated, legalistic procedures. This causes many cases to focus on the form, rather than the substance, of a pleading or of a proposed response to a change in the environment of the regulated.

5. The collegial form exacerbates the problem of accountability by providing considerable anonymity to individual decision makers. Neither the Congress, the President, nor the public can pinpoint the responsibility for a particular decision.

In sum, regulatory agencies have been constructed to resemble high-level, collegial courts, and it is not surprising to the Ash Council that they appear to behave like these courts, emphasizing procedures and dealing with individual cases. But agencies also make policy and rules of behavior that are the guides for the cases they adjudicate. The Ash report concludes that the collegial form prevents the agencies from performing the latter function effectively.

Review of Decisions

Cases before regulatory commissions go through three stages before a decision is final. First, a hearing examiner—a civil service employee—collects information pertinent to the case, hears the pleadings of the parties at interest, and, depending on the agency, either makes a provisional decision or recommends a decision to the commission. Certainly if the parties to the case are dissatisfied with the result, and often if they are not dissatisfied, the commission also examines the case. Finally, after the commission reaches a decision, the parties to the case may appeal the decision to the federal courts, either on the grounds that proper procedures were not followed at some stage of the information-gathering and decision-making processes or on the grounds that the decision is contradicted by the laws and executive orders defining the authority of the agency.

The Ash Council sees three flaws in this system. First, the process is slow and cumbersome. At each stage essentially the same ground is covered, with essentially the same expensive and time-consuming procedures being followed. This duplication of effort wastes the time of the agency staff, the commissioners, the courts, and the parties to regulatory cases. Second, the position of the hearing examiner is made less attractive since the process strips him of any real authority. In important, controversial cases his input is unlikely to be very important since both commissioners and judges will reevaluate all the material pertinent to the case. Third, at some stage a decision by a commissioner or a judge is likely to be made from ignorance. Since the case-by-case, formalistic approach to regulation overburdens the system with work, decision makers are likely to be less than well informed on a particular case. The problem is compounded by the fact that the federal courts to which agency decisions are appealed deal with the full array of criminal, civil, and administrative cases. It is unrealistic to expect federal judges to be experts in all fields, particularly in view of the large and growing number of cases of all kinds pending in the courts.

Divisions of Responsibility among Agencies

Regulatory agencies have developed primarily as a series of ad hoc responses to specific public policy problems. They are not the result of a clearly delineated theory of the role of government in business decisions, nor of a coherent plan for extending government influence into private economic decisions. The Ash Council holds the view that the resulting allocation of responsibilities to regulatory agencies has created two major types of problems.

First, the decisions of one agency often alter the results of the decisions of another agency since the issues or individuals the two agencies are called upon to regulate are often strongly interrelated. An obvious example that is discussed at length in the report is the division among three agencies of the responsibility for regulating transportation. Another example mentioned by the Council is the responsibility of the Federal Power Commission and the Securities and Exchange Commission in dealing with public utility holding companies.

Second, individual regulatory agencies are often given responsibilities that cause institutional schizophrenia within the agency. Several agencies are instructed to promote the development of an industry as well as to regulate it in the interest of the general public. The most obvious example is the power of the Civil Aeronautics Board (CAB) to set rates, award routes, and provide subsidies for local service airlines. The Ash Council believes that regulation and promotion are incompatible since they are often conflicting. In other cases, agencies are saddled with a hodge-podge of unrelated responsibilities that prevent the agency from having a focus or clearly defined mission. The prime example cited by the Council is the Federal Trade Commission. The Ash Council believes that the FTC's consumer protection responsibilities are

fundamentally different from its antitrust responsibilities. The Council concludes that regulation in both areas would be more effective if each were the
sole responsibility of one agency.

The Cure: Restructure the Regulatory System

The Ash Council proposes four major changes in the structure of regulation: limit the number of commissioners as much as possible—in most cases
replacing a commission with a single administrator; make regulation more
responsive to the political system by making the heads of regulatory agencies
(single administrators or commissioners) members of the President's administration; increase the efficiency of the process of deciding individual cases by
limiting internal agency review and by creating a special Administrative Court;
and rationalize the distribution of functions and responsibilities among agencies. The specific proposals of the Council are as follows:

Rationalizing Responsibility

1. The three principal transportation agencies, the Interstate Commerce
Commission, the Civil Aeronautics Board, and the Federal Maritime Commission, should be merged into a single Transportation Regulatory Agency.

2. The Federal Trade Commission should be divided into two agencies, a
Federal Trade Practices Agency to deal with consumer protection and a Federal
Antitrust Board to assume the FTC's responsibilities in antitrust enforcement.

3. Promotional responsibilities should not be given to regulatory agencies
and should be transferred to an appropriate executive department. Specifically,
the CAB's program of subsidies for local service airlines should be transferred
to the Department of Transportation.

4. Administration of the Public Utility Holding Company Act should be
transferred from the Securities and Exchange Commission to the Federal
Power Agency.

Restructuring the Agency

1. The agencies responsible for regulating transportation, securities, power,
and trade practices should be headed by a single administrator, serving at the
pleasure of the President.

2. A new three-member Federal Antitrust Board should be established. The
chairman should have the responsibility of managing the agency and establishing priorities. The two remaining members should be economists, one the
director of economic analysis within the agency and the other a member of

the Council of Economic Advisers. All three would serve at the pleasure of the President and would be appointed subject to Senate confirmation. The highly unusual size and professional composition of the proposed Board are desirable, according to the Ash Council, because of the need to bolster the role of economic analysis in antitrust enforcement and to insure the coordination of antitrust efforts with general economic policy.

3. The Federal Communications Commission should remain roughly as it is now, the only change being a reduction in the number of commissioners from seven to five. The Ash Council asserts that the responsibilities of the FCC in regulating broadcasting necessitate special safeguards against domination by a single individual, either the President or a single administrator, who might use his authority to promote a particular political ideology.

Reforming Review

1. A time limit—perhaps thirty days—should be placed on the delay between a preliminary decision by a hearing examiner and review by an agency head (single administrator or commission). At the end of the grace period, the hearing examiner's decision would automatically become the final agency position. Agency directors would then be in a position only to examine a selected sample of cases decided by a hearing examiner. Furthermore, agency directors should be required to explain the basis for remanding an examiner's decision when they chose to do so, citing specifically how the decision was inconsistent with agency policy.

2. An Administrative Court should be established, responsible only for reviewing the decisions of regulatory agencies. The Court would be concerned principally with the procedures of the agencies and would work toward spreading worthwhile procedural innovations from one agency to another. The Court should not have a fixed venue, but should make periodic appearances throughout the nation. Approximately fifteen judges would be needed for administrative review. These should be appointed by the President, subject to Senate confirmation, for long terms—perhaps fifteen years. One judge should be designated as Chief Judge and should be responsible for organizing and supervising the Court and assigning cases.

Alternatives Considered

The Ash Council, aware of the revolutionary character of its proposals, considered several lesser reforms, but rejected each as inadequate. The report mentions five alternatives and the reasons for rejecting each.

1. *Retaining the independent collegial bodies, but reducing the number of commissioners.* Fewer commissioners would mean a less protracted search for consensus among a majority, and hence less delay and less reliance on procedures and the case method. The Ash Council believes that this proposal does not go far enough; one commissioner would be the ideal number, and any larger number would mean a substantial reduction in efficiency.

2. *Placing all administrative functions, including policy formulation, in the hands of the chairman and limiting the role of the commission to reviewing cases.* Because the chairman would have to obtain commission agreement on general agency policy in order for case decisions to be consistent, this proposal would do little to remove the current need for consensus on policy formulation. There appears to be no way to provide a chairman with "undiluted authority" to manage an agency.

3. *Placing administrative functions and case review in the hands of the chairman and leaving policy formulation to the commission.* The Ash Council believes that the main advantage of this proposal is that it gives an administrator and a commission "those functions for which each is best suited." Unfortunately, as a practical matter, the Council believes that case review and agency management (defining priorities and staff assignments) cannot be separated from policy formation. The authority to decide cases is, in the end, the authority to make policy. Giving commissions both policy formulation and case review authority, but giving the chairman sole responsibility for administration, would probably be the only workable arrangement, according to the Council; however, this would not go far enough since long delays in policy formulation would still occur.

4. *Creating a commission on commissions to oversee appointments to commissions.* The "commission on commissions" proposal is an attempt to find a solution to the problem that most commissioners are of less than first-rate quality—at least in the eyes of many observers. The Ash Council believes that this reform would treat an effect rather than a cause. According to the Council, no one can perform the job of commissioner well due to organizational difficulties within the agency and in the entire federal establishment. This reduces the attractiveness of the job to first-rate people and causes the President to give less thought to appointments to regulatory commissions. The result is commissioners of uneven ability and spotty performances by the regulatory agencies. The formation of a supercommission would not change the agencies nor the job of a commissioner; therefore, it would not be likely to have a significant effect on the quality of either commissioners or agency performance. Presumably only a job that is rewarding to an able person would end up being filled by an able person.

5. *Establishing a commission to resolve cases in which agency jurisdictions overlap.* The proposal, while improving coordination of policies among agencies, further fragments regulatory responsibility, and creates still another source of delay in reaching policy decisions. The Ash Council sees the disadvantages far outweighing the advantages.

Controversial Issues in the Ash Report

The remaining chapters of this paper deal with several problems of regulation that the Ash Council report considered only summarily—or not at all. The more important controversial positions taken in the report are briefly discussed in the remaining pages of this chapter.

The Factual and Analytical Basis of the Report

Perhaps the most outstanding characteristic of the Ash Council report is the absence of factual or analytical evidence for most of the conclusions reached by the Council about both the principal failings of regulation and the cause of these failings. The Ash Council gives the impression that it believes that the main problems of regulation are the delay in making decisions and the absence of clear policy guidelines to the regulated industries. A third problem is the failure to coordinate policies across agencies; another is an overemphasis of legal issues, with an underemphasis of economic and engineering evidence. The causes of these problems are said to be independent status, collegial structure, and inefficient review.

The report mentions only once, and then dismisses as an organizational problem, the most common complaint, that in formulating policy and deciding cases, regulatory agencies pay too little attention to the interests of the general public and of consumers and too much attention to the interests of industry. The report does not mention at all the more basic complaint that regulation has acted to restrain competition. Regulators have acted to preserve the market shares of existing firms and industries by preventing competition in areas where competition is workable, desirable, and incipient. The report does not deal with the substantial body of literature that cites instances of unwarranted interference by the Congress and the executive in regulatory decisions. This literature, of course, controverts the Council's assumption that the agencies are really independent of, and lack accountability to, the politically sensitive arms of government. Finally, the report makes no attempt to evaluate the performance of numerous regulatory agencies for which the Council offers no reform proposals. The most obvious omissions from the report's evaluations and recommendations are the National Labor Relations Board (an independent commission), the Federal Aviation Administration, the Food and Drug Administration, the Antitrust division of the Department of Justice, and the agencies responsible for regulating the banking industry. The organization and position within the government of several of these agencies is very similar to the new arrangements proposed for the agencies examined by the Council. Should one assume that regulation is relatively problem-free in these other agencies?

The Ash Council is critical of the Congress for establishing a chain of regulatory agencies without a specific plan and political theory in mind, but the Council's conclusions are often based on ad hoc judgments. For example, the report does not reveal the political theory that led the Council to conclude that greater presidential authority, rather than greater congressional authority, would increase the sensitivity of regulatory agencies to the general public interest in regulation, or, for that matter, that either would be more effective than the shield of independence.

Form and Function Separated

The Ash report does not discuss a fundamental problem—that most regulatory agencies were established through bad legislation that did not adequately define the role and responsibility of regulators. The chairman of the Council gives a clue why this issue was not dealt with by the Council in his transmittal letter to the President. He says that the issues of the *structure* of regulation must be decided before attention can be focused on the *scope* of regulation.[2] The Council evidently has assumed that the choices of an effective organizational structure and of the relationship of the regulatory establishment to the rest of government can be largely independent of the purposes and methods of regulation.[3] Thus, whether the laws delegating regulatory responsibilities to the agencies are clear or vague, narrow or broad, the same principles apply in designing the organization of regulation.

This conclusion is, of course, debatable and is to some extent contradicted by the Council's own decisions to propose no reforms for the National Labor

2. The letter says: "Although the regulatory laws may need revision, changes in regulatory structure can and indeed should be implemented in advance of changes in the substantive laws. The existing structure, because of its inherent and perhaps unavoidable deficiencies, cannot be expected to accommodate these revised mandates. . . . A more effective and objective regulatory process, better integrated with other processes of government, requires a new organizational framework for regulation." (The President's Advisory Council on Executive Organization, *A New Regulatory Framework: Report on Selected Independent Regulatory Agencies* [1971], p. iii.)

3. The Ash Council is aware that this assumption is not necessarily valid, as was indicated by the chairman in his transmittal letter: "Due attention should be given to differences in the responsibilities of the regulatory agencies in evaluating these proposals. For while we have emphasized similarity in our findings, others may, in noting differences, arrive at divergent conclusions." (*Ibid.*, p. iv.)

Relations Board and only minor reforms for the Federal Communications Commission.

The Political Realities

The Council cannot be faulted for making the proposals it deemed best, regardless of political feasibility. Nevertheless, it is surprising that the Council did not mention the long-standing defensiveness of the Congress about turning over to the President any significant responsibility for regulation. The Council report contains a detailed list of all the past presidential commissions whose similar proposals to incorporate regulation into the executive structure have fallen by the wayside, but no commentary on whether congressional fears are unwarranted or how the new recommendations avoid some of the problems the Congress has had with previous proposals.

The Short List of Alternatives

The final controversial aspect of the Ash Council report is the meager list of alternative reforms of the regulatory system that were presented and discussed by the Council. Among the alternatives that certainly deserve consideration and that are worthy of comparison with the Ash Council proposals are:

1. The Landis proposal to create an executive office with a single administrator responsible for all regulatory policy; regulatory agencies would operate under the direction of the "czar."[4]

2. The Lowi proposal to rewrite the legislation establishing regulatory agencies to make their responsibilities and authority clearly delineated, following the example of the 1887 Interstate Commerce Act rather than the 1920 Transportation Act.[5]

3. The "continuing reevaluation" proposal to establish a procedure by which regulatory agencies, and/or the congressional subcommittees overseeing them, would be required to prepare regular reports on the policies and effectiveness of the regulatory agency in each of its areas of responsibility.[6]

4. "Give-up-the-ghost" proposals—either to deregulate all or some regulated industries (on the grounds that competition is adequate, at least in comparison with the effectiveness of regulation) or to nationalize them (on the grounds that only then can the schizophrenia over profits and public interest be dealt with).

4. James M. Landis, *Report on Regulatory Agencies to the President-Elect* (1960).

5. Theodore J. Lowi, *The End of Liberalism: Ideology, Policy, and the Crisis of Public Authority* (Norton, 1969).

6. See Henry J. Friendly, *The Federal Administrative Agencies: The Need for Better Definition of Standards* (Harvard University Press, 1962).

CHAPTER THREE

THE FAILINGS OF REGULATION

The Ash Council was not asked to express its opinion on the proper role of regulation in society and the objectives of regulatory policy. Consequently, the Council focused on the inability of regulatory agencies to achieve whatever objectives happen to be established, either by regulators or by the Congress. Whatever mistakes regulatory agencies make are assumed to flow from the organizational structure of regulation, which causes decisions to be ex post facto, delayed, and based on incomplete information. If agencies have better information, more coordination, and a streamlined decision-making process, the failings of regulation will disappear, since regulators, it is assumed, do strive to act in the public interest.

An alternative view is that the performance of regulatory agencies is unsatisfactory because regulators have chosen to pursue objectives that are contrary to the public interest. (If this is true, of course, improving the ability of regulatory authorities to attain their objectives could make matters worse.) On a number of important issues, considerable expert support can be found for the view that regulatory agencies have defined for themselves policy objectives that can be construed as sacrificing the public interest to the interests of the regulated.

The term "public interest" can be so vague that it is devoid of meaning. In this monograph it refers to the policies government would pursue if it gave equal weight to the welfare of every member of society. In regulation the global public interest is normally composed of the employees and owners of regulated firms and the purchasers of the services these firms provide. To say that regulation is excessively sensitive to the interests of regulated firms and therefore acts against the public interest is to say, in essence, that regulators pay too little attention to the interests of consumers. Since no technique is available for comparing the welfare of different individuals, the performance of regulatory agencies is judged herein by the extent to which their actions correct for the market failures that were the motivation for establishing regulation. Among these market failures are monopoly inequities and inefficiencies and the information problems associated with certain goods and services with characteristics, purposes, or effects that are difficult to understand. As President Nixon remarked when the Ash Council report was released to the public, regulation should "protect the members of the consuming public against market abuses over which they [have] little control."

The following pages examine several issues of regulatory policies and practices (some briefly discussed in the Ash Council report) that can provide useful evidence for evaluating the two alternative views of regulation. None of the issues is relevant to each of the entire heterogeneous collection of regulatory agencies and responsibilities. They obviously apply only to regulation in a general sense. Certainly, not all agencies have the same kinds of responsibilities, and some decisions are more in the public interest than others. Nevertheless, generalizations are offered because decisions of agencies in a wide variety of circumstances seem roughly to fit a particular pattern.

Price Regulation

Economists have been highly critical of the methods and objectives of regulatory commissions in regulating prices. Economists see prices as guides to efficient resource allocation, providing the owners of the nation's productive agents—labor, machines, natural resources—with incentives to produce a combination of goods and services that maximizes consumer welfare. The price system can serve this function only if each price is a measure of all of the costs—private and social—of producing one more unit of output—the incremental or marginal cost.

Regulators tend to view a given price as part of a general price structure, the purpose of which is to generate enough revenue to cover costs, including allowable profits. In the eyes of regulators, an individual price is not closely related to either the cost or the social value of the service it covers. Regulatory policy might accurately be characterized as maximizing the size of the regulated industry, subject to the requirement that a firm's total revenues cover total costs and provide a return on investment that the agencies regard as reasonable. Guaranteeing the provision of a specific service to a specific locality and assuring the continued viability of an existing firm or industry are often related objectives of regulation. The price structure is the vehicle for achieving these ends.

Cross-Subsidization

One major use of the price system by regulators is to charge prices above incremental costs for some services to offset losses of other services due to prices that are set below incremental cost. Cross-subsidization is particularly common in public utility regulation. Telephone service, electric power, and transportation are all priced with cross-subsidization in mind.[1]

Example: airline fares.[2] The Civil Aeronautics Board (CAB) has tried to set fares on high-density and long-distance routes substantially above costs, so that the excess revenue from these routes can be used to subsidize service to smaller cities with very little traffic.[3] The justification by the CAB for its pricing policy is that a complete network of airline routes is more in the national interest than efficient pricing. Critics contend that passengers on high-profit routes, who have no greater interest than does society in general in subsidizing service to localities with little traffic, should not bear the burden of the subsidy. They point to the Los Angeles-San Francisco market, an intra-state route not subject to CAB price regulation, that has a $16.50 airfare for a 340-mile flight, compared to a $26 fare for the 230-mile flight between New York City and Washington, D.C. The CAB contends that if all routes with high profit potential were competitive, only a small fraction of the nation's cities would have air service.

Critics also point out that in the long run the CAB policy is usually self-defeating. Price reductions are not the only available means for competing. When three or four airlines are awarded the right to serve an over-priced route, they compete through improving services, such as more stewardesses per passenger, better (free) meals, more frequent flights with a lower percentage of occupied seats, and new aircraft that are introduced before they are economically justified. Service competition raises the costs per passenger of air service on the high-profit runs. The CAB must in turn grant fare increases—

1. The Ash report criticizes cross-subsidization in transportation as an uneconomical distribution of services among modes and because it "may have detrimental spillover effects." But it attributes the problem to the division of transport regulation among three independent agencies. See The President's Advisory Council on Executive Organization, *A New Regulatory Framework: Report on Selected Independent Regulatory Agencies* (1971), pp. 70-71. The report does not discuss similar policies of other agencies responsible for regulating prices.

2. See George Eads, "The Local Service Airline 'Experiment' After Twenty-Five Years: An Assessment" (study in preparation for the Brookings Institution), and Richard E. Caves, *Air Transport and Its Regulators: An Industry Study* (Harvard University Press, 1962).

3. In general, the costs per passenger per mile flown are lower the longer the route and the greater the number of passengers flown. Airline fares, however, are nearly proportional to distance and almost independent of the average number of passengers flown.

despite substantial excess capacity—so that the cross-subsidization from the high-profit routes can continue.

The CAB policy is more beneficial to the industry than a policy of cost-related prices would be, but less so than a completely passive policy that would permit the industry to behave as a cartel. Like other regulatory agencies, the CAB has responded to its mandate to control monopoly profits by controlling the relationship between profits and costs. Airlines are permitted to earn profits equal to a fixed percentage of their capital investment. Thus they can increase their profits only by increasing their investments. High fares on the potentially most profitable routes lead to increases in total airline investment. Competition through service increases the number of planes flown on the high-profit routes; the remaining excess profits are used to offset the losses of flying more planes on unprofitable routes. The monopoly revenues of the high-profit route still tend to be collected, but are partly dissipated in the increased costs to the firm of providing unremunerative services. The firm thereby earns more profits than it would if competition dictated which routes were served, but less than if a cartelized industry dispensed with both losing routes and excess capacity (and continued to charge monopoly prices on the profitable routes).

Protection of a Particular Industry or Firm

Regulatory agencies also use minimum price regulation to prevent low-cost industries or firms from capturing business from high-cost actual or potential competitors.

Example: surface transport. Railroads, water carriers, and trucking firms[4] ordinarily face entirely different costs for providing a given service in a given area. If boats, trucks, and trains were used to best advantage, each would charge prices related to the cost of the service provided, and every shipment would be sent by the least costly mode. Yet the Interstate Commerce Commission (ICC), in an attempt to preserve for each mode some of the market for each service, often sets prices for all modes at roughly the costs of the highest-cost mode. The most common application of this policy is to prevent the railroads from lowering prices to the level of incremental costs and thereby capturing much of the long-distance shipping business from trucks. This practice, like cross-subsidization, is defended on the grounds that the national interest demands a "balanced" transportation system that gives as many shippers as possible a choice of modes. Often the specter of monopolization by a firm is transferred to the idea of monopolization by mode; for example, a

4. See Ann F. Friedlaender, *The Dilemma of Freight Transport Regulation* (Brookings Institution, 1969).

price decision will be said to prevent monopolization of a particular service by trucks or by railroads.

The argument against this practice is simply that regulation prevents the benefits of a low-cost technology from being realized by consumers in the form of lower prices and by the low-cost firm in the form of new business. If the national interest requires the continuation of a service that transport customers do not want to use, the burden of maintaining it should be spread more widely than just among those customers.

The National Interest in Price Regulation

Regulators are not necessarily wrong in their approach to price regulation. They might agree that the most effective means for preserving services, industries, and firms—if preservation is in the national interest—is a general subsidy; however, the regulators could quickly point out that the Congress has not voted such a subsidy, except for local service airlines and the maritime industry, and that meanwhile the next best solution is to use the price structure to subsidize the unviable services. If the economically unviable services are highly valued, then the costs of an inefficient price structure are worth bearing.

Critics of price regulation reply that the national interest in subsidizing unremunerative services has not been established either by persuasive argument or by legislation, and that regulators have no reason to believe that society does benefit from the structure of regulated industries that the regulatory agencies have promulgated. In many cases, policies designed to benefit the regulated firms have, without justification, been identified with the national interest in order to deflect criticism.

If an important purpose of regulation is to guarantee that certain firms, industries, and services continue to be economically viable through protection against lower cost competition, then price regulation is not a failure, except in the case of the railroads. If, on the other hand, the main purpose of regulation is to protect the consumer against the abuses of monopoly, by fostering competition where possible and by simulating it through price regulation elsewhere, then regulation has failed—not because of ineffectiveness, but because of misdirection.

Franchise Awards

A major function of many regulatory agencies is to control market entry and exit of regulated firms. The Federal Communications Commission (FCC) controls access to the part of the electromagnetic spectrum that is not reserved for the federal government, the transportation agencies grant rights to provide service on a given route, and the Federal Power Commission (FPC) confers the right to provide wholesale power and natural gas.

Franchising and Price Regulation

The licensing function is closely related to price regulation, since the price structure can be used to subsidize nonremunerative services only if regulators can decide how many and which firms can participate in an overpriced market. Thus the airlines permitted to fly overpriced routes are also required to fly nonremunerative, low-density routes; meanwhile, airlines that, in the absence of regulation, would respond to the high prices on the lucrative routes by entering the market and charging lower fares are prevented from doing so. With minor qualifications, these licensing decisions are in the public interest only if price regulation as practiced is in the public interest.

Franchising without Price Regulation

Some licensing responsibilities are not accompanied by price regulation. Local governments engage in this type of franchising to a much greater extent than does the federal government; perhaps the most notorious example is the awarding of taxi medallions in several large cities.[5] Federal franchising that is unrelated to price regulation takes place primarily outside of regulatory agencies. Executive agencies, for example, sell logging rights in national forests, concession rights in national parks, and grazing rights on federal lands. The regulatory agencies that the Ash Council examined have two major licensing functions in this category: granting permits for constructing hydroelectric power facilities (FPC) and allocating electromagnetic frequencies for communications use (FCC). In addition, two kinds of franchises are granted by independent regulatory agencies the Ash Council did not examine: the Atomic Energy Commission (AEC) licenses the construction of nuclear reactors, such as for use in atomic power plants, and several agencies grant licenses to operate federally chartered financial institutions.

The principal criticism of licensing that is unrelated to price regulation is that licensing agencies give too much consideration to the interests of the license applicant and not enough to society generally. The most commonly heard complaints are that insufficient attention is paid to important issues affecting the general welfare—such as environmental effects—and that the licensing responsibility is used to limit competition.

5. For an interesting discussion of how local government can make a competitive industry monopolistic, see Edmund W. Kitch, "The Regulation of Taxicabs in the City of Chicago, Illinois," *Journal of Law and Economics* (to be published in October 1971).

Example: broadcast licensing. The FCC is explicitly prevented by the Communications Act of 1934 from regulating prices and profits in broadcasting.[6] Its sole responsibility is to allocate radio frequencies in the public interest. Critics of the FCC's licensing policies focus on the agency's definition of the public interest in broadcasting. The FCC, believing in localism, divides the small number of prime very high frequency (VHF) television assignments among adjacent cities for allocation to relatively weak stations with largely duplicative programming. This is regarded as more in the public interest than permitting more powerful regional stations that would offer viewers more program options in this prime spectrum space. The FCC does not insist that licensees produce much programming with anything except commercial appeal for advertisers in mind. The FCC does not, and probably could not legally, exercise extensive control over program content (though the Ash Council mistakenly states that it does); however, it is permitted to require public-service programming and to enforce the "fairness doctrine," which is supposed to guarantee the rights of both sides in a political debate to be heard. But the FCC has required only minimal public service broadcasting and has made little effort to use its licensing power to influence the decisions of licensees with respect to programming.

The FCC policy is defended on the grounds that government should never interfere with the mass communications media, for to do so is to threaten the democratic process. To require public service programming would necessitate defining public service, which, say the defenders, would confer an enormous power over the information flow within society. Critics respond that to require broadcasters to devote a small fraction of prime viewing time to socially beneficial programming is not the same as to insist on full government control of program content. Furthermore, the FCC's conception of satisfactory public interest goals seems remarkably consistent with the profitability goals of the broadcaster.[7] Localism limits competition, and the lack of significant public service requirements allows nearly all broadcast time to be commercially oriented. Finally, the FCC's historical "squatter's rights" attitude toward license renewals and transfers protects the existing industry. In essence, a challenge to a license renewal has been successful in the past only if the challenger could prove that the license holder was especially derelict in serving the community. Recently the commission has become somewhat more receptive to challenges to license renewals, yet the FCC still maintains that there is little

6. 48 Stat. 1065.

7. Harvey J. Levin estimates that as much as 60 percent of the sales price of broadcasting stations is the capitalized value of the license ("Economic Effects of Broadcast Licensing," *Journal of Political Economy*, Vol. 72 [April 1964], p. 157).

point in having competition based on general programming plans—such as the fraction of time the station intends to devote to noncommercial, educational, and public affairs programming—since once a license is granted the licensee can do as he pleases. But the FCC could make other rules. More specific statements of a station's intended mix of programming could be required, and licensees who did not fulfill promises about the amount of public service programming to be offered could have their licenses canceled or made unrenewable.[8]

The Public Interest in Licensing

Price regulation that seeks to preserve abnormally high profits to be used to cross-subsidize unremunerative services cannot succeed without parallel regulation of entry into the high-profit service. Some licensing by regulatory agencies is designed to prevent competition and thereby preserve the funds for cross-subsidization. Licensing in conjunction with price regulation is valid only to the extent that price regulation itself is justified. If subsidization through price regulation is not in the public interest, then both price regulation and franchising should be dispensed with in potentially competitive markets.

Franchising that is not connected to price regulation and that limits competition is not necessarily against the public interest. Preventing individuals from trying to broadcast on the same frequency, limiting the number of dams that can be constructed on a scenically attractive river, or ensuring that only a minimum amount of commercial development takes place in a national park are all legitimate social objectives. In these cases the purpose of franchising is not to create lucrative monopoly rights that will produce high profits for the lucky recipient of a franchise; rather the goal is to serve a public end that is related to the number of firms permitted to do business or to use a resource. In these cases the government can and should capture the monopoly profits from the franchise right by selling the franchise to the highest bidder who can promise a satisfactory performance. The highest bid will leave to the licensee the profits necessary to induce him to use a resource or enter an industry, but

8. The license renewal process is currently being changed by the FCC. The main components of the new system will be wider publication of the extent of public service broadcasting by stations, automatic investigation of the renewal applications of only the very worst stations, and simpler procedures for lodging and evidentially supporting public complaints against a renewal applicant. But a formal statement of what constitutes adequate service, or a procedure whereby licenses might change hands more freely, is apparently not in the cards. For an explanation of the new procedures, see Federal Communications Commission, FCC 71-156: 58741; 71-59: 58744; and 71-176: 58786.

will not provide additional profits arising from the licensee's insulation from competition.[9]

In a few cases the government does sell franchises—for example, lumbering rights in national forests. Independent regulatory agencies have uniformly rejected the auction method of granting licenses, regardless of the relationship of the license to the agency's price regulation authority and policy.

While entry limitation without price regulation can be justified in principle, there is considerable controversy over whether such policy is in the public interest in many areas where it is practiced. Entry limits in broadcasting go beyond what is necessary to prevent interference. In banking (a regulated activity not examined by the Ash Council) any limitation on the number of nationally chartered banks and savings institutions in a given locality is certainly a highly questionable policy, especially since federal regulations governing banking practices and insurance of deposits substantially reduce, if not eliminate, whatever consumer risks freer competition would create. This type of entry limitation represents perhaps the most extreme example of regulation that serves the interests of the regulated industry at the expense of the public interest. It insulates the licensee from competition when such insulation provides no benefits to society, and then refuses to collect at least some of the artificially created excess profits through auctioning of licenses among qualified potential licensees.

Influencing Technological Change

By controlling prices, profits, and entry, regulatory agencies also control regulated firms' choice of technology. The Ash Council recognizes that regulation has inhibited the timely adoption of new technology, but blames this on the delays in the regulatory process and the insulation of the agencies from the general economic system. Implicit in the Ash Council's assessment is the view that regulators do want beneficial technological change to proceed, but that they have a very difficult time learning about promising technologies and deciding how they should be used.

9. For an examination of the feasibility and desirability of selling broadcasting licenses, see Ronald Coase, "The Federal Communications Commission," *Journal of Law and Economics,* Vol. 2 (October 1959). For a colloquium on the same issue, see Harvey J. Levin, "Spectrum Allocation Without Market" and "Comments" by Alfred E. Kahn, Roger G. Noll, William H. Meckling, and William K. Jones, under "Discussion" in American Economic Association, *Papers and Proceedings of the Eighty-second Annual Meeting, 1969, American Economic Review,* Vol. 60 (May 1970), pp. 209-24.

Another view is that regulatory agencies intentionally delay or prevent many beneficial technological changes.[10] According to this view, agencies have inhibited the development of a number of promising technologies, while promoting others that were not beneficial. When regulation leads to a choice of technology that benefits no one, not even the regulated industry, the Ash Council's view is plausible. But such is not always the case.

Regulatory agencies have delayed or prevented a number of technological changes that threatened either to shift substantial business from one regulated firm or industry to another or to result in substantially less profit for regulated firms generally. The agencies most often guilty of such choices are the ICC and the FCC—for example, in impeding use of the Big John hopper railroad car, prohibiting foreign attachments on the switched communications network, and restricting the development of pay TV. All of these are examples of a long regulatory delay, for eventually the regulatory agencies did permit the new technological development.

Example: truck-rail piggybacking. In the piggybacking case the ICC chose to permit some technological progress, but not nearly as much as would have been possible. Rail Form A, which specifies the minimum revenues that a railroad flatcar must earn when fully loaded, was applied to any form of flatcar used to carry the cargo of a truck. When the railroads introduced piggybacking, they had a two-dimensional choice of technologies. First was the length of the flatcar. Should it carry one or two truck trailers? Second was the part of the truck to be carried. Should the entire trailer be carried or just the freight container? The lowest-cost solution for many railroads was to carry only the containers on cars built for one truckload. Securing a container to a car is less expensive than securing an entire trailer. The shorter car is more stable on sharply curving or banked road beds, can manage the sharpest turns inside tunnels without scraping the side of the tunnel, is compatible with existing railyard switching equipment, and requires no excess capacity when an odd number of trucks are carried. (The capital costs per unit of capacity are slightly higher for the shorter car, but not enough to offset the other advantages for many railroads.) The railroads cannot adopt the low-cost option, for the ICC insists that all flatcars, regardless of length, must satisfy the Form A revenue requirements. Hence the price charged on the single-truck car must be twice the price charged on the two-truck car, despite the cost advantages of the former. Furthermore, since flatcars, regardless of length, cannot have different prices for containers than for whole trailers, the truck-

10. For a far more complete treatment of the effects of regulation on technological progress, see William M. Capron (ed.), *Technological Change in Regulated Industries* (Brookings Institution, 1971).

ing industry has no incentive to use containers, although the cost of switching to containers would have been well worth the saving in transport costs. The piggyback innovation has thereby been partly, but not wholly, inhibited; rails have not captured as much traffic from long-distance trucking and waterways as they otherwise would have, and traditional modal shares in transportation have been upset less than would otherwise have been the case. The main loser was the consumer, since commodity prices must include unnecessarily high transportation costs.

Socially Optimal Technological Change

The process by which new technology is adopted differs widely between regulated and unregulated sectors. Normally in an unregulated industry new technology is adopted because it gives a firm a market advantage, either through lower costs and prices or through increases in quality at a cost consumers are willing to bear. This process is often disruptive, changing substantially the market shares and profitability of firms within an industry. The value of existing capital assets, and hence the wealth of firm owners, is often drastically altered by technological change. But usually a technological innovation spreads quickly through an industry, giving only a temporary advantage to the innovating firm. In many of the industries in which technological change is most rapid, the distribution of wealth within the industry does not appear to be changing drastically.

Regulatory agencies pay a great deal of attention to the effect of a potential innovation on the distribution of wealth within an industry. No matter how beneficial an innovation, it has little chance of timely adoption in a regulated industry if it will lead to a substantial redistribution of wealth among the regulated that cannot be compensated through some clever regulatory device. Regulatory agencies take this position because of two highly controversial attitudes that they tend to share.

The sunk cost obsession. Regulatory agencies abhor abandoning a capital investment—a rail line, a transoceanic cable—as long as it is in good working order and has not been fully depreciated by the owner. They commonly regard the cost of an innovation as the direct cost of introducing it plus the book value of the assets it will make obsolete. The innovation must be sufficiently profitable to earn the allowed rate of return on its own investment plus the remaining book value of the replaced capital. This procedure, of course, neglects all the consumer benefits of the innovation.

A spectacular illustration of how misleading this approach can be is the decision to authorize a fifth transatlantic communications cable (TAT-5), rather than a satellite, to meet the growing demand for communications services across the Atlantic.[11] The costs per circuit on the new cable were lower than for past cables, but considerably higher than for satellites. Unfortunately this could not be reflected in prices. The new cable, being owned by owners of the other cables, would lower transatlantic communications prices by lowering the capital investment per circuit on cables, and thus the price of a cable circuit. The satellite, owned by the Communications Satellite Corporation (Comsat), would not lower the average cost of a cable circuit; furthermore the Atlantic satellite system would have to continue to subsidize losses on the Pacific system. Hence the lower costs of satellites would not lead to lower transatlantic communications prices. (Previously the FCC had ensured this particular perverse price behavior through the authorized-user decision, which prevented Comsat from selling its services directly to the public. All of the firms authorized by the FCC to provide international common carrier communications service also own the cables. These firms decide whether to route a communications connection by cable or by satellite.) To be sure, the TAT-5 decision will produce lower prices for transatlantic telephone calls than would have a decision to authorize a satellite; however, if prices had been permitted to reflect true costs on each mode and competition had been used to determine the successful technology, satellites would have replaced cables for most communications uses. Because of the ownership structure of the international communications industry, this would have caused a substantial redistribution of wealth and might even have put one firm—Western Union International—out of business. Promotion of an inferior technology prevented this from happening.

The distaste for uncertainty. The second reason for the reluctance of regulatory agencies to encourage technological change is the belief that regulators should reduce as much as possible the uncertainty faced by regulated firms. Regulators believe that since regulation limits profits and constrains other business decisions of firms, something must be given in return. Not only would it be inequitable for regulation to add to uncertainty, it would also be unfair to restrain profits and dictate the type of service that firms must provide unless firms were insulated from some of the possibilities of financial loss. Regulators also believe that consumers benefit from the reduced uncertainty in the regulated sector: there is "social value in encouraging the security of transactions."[12]

Both positions have some validity. Generally individuals prefer to avoid

11. See Merton J. Peck, "The Single-Entity Proposal for International Telecommunications," in American Economic Association, *Papers and Proceedings of the Eighty-second Annual Meeting, 1969, American Economic Review,* Vol. 60 (May 1970), pp. 199-203.

12. Henry J. Friendly, *The Federal Administrative Agencies: The Need for Better Definition of Standards* (Harvard University Press, 1962), p. 20.

risk, and risky businesses normally must have a higher profit potential to attract investment. Other things being equal, allowed profits in the regulated sector should be higher if regulated firms are to assume greater risk. Furthermore, public utilities are so vital to the operation of society that continuity of service has great value. Nevertheless, the attempt to reduce uncertainty substantially has serious disadvantages because of its effect on innovation. Firms in the industry cannot count on obtaining permission to use a new technology. Their markets are under less of a threat from potential competitors, so that they need not worry as much either about making capital investments that may not be justified by the demand for services or about the possibility that new technology might make their investments obsolete before the costs have been fully recouped. In any event, the amount of their investments will remain in the rate base, and prices for other services can be adjusted to guarantee the overall rate of return of the firm.

Regulatory agencies probably overstate the case for reducing uncertainty in relation to both the profit-limitation and the service-continuity arguments. Regulation limits profits because the dominant market position of firms subject to regulation would otherwise lead to abnormally large profits. Regulated firms are generally limited to an after-tax rate of profit on capital investment of 8 to 9 percent, which is not much below the average for U.S. industry of about 10 percent. A few regulated firms are permitted much higher returns. Comsat, for example, has proposed an 11 percent after-tax return on a domestic satellite system, and local service airlines have been permitted, although they seldom actually realize, a 14 percent after-tax return. Regulated firms are all permitted substantially higher returns than are offered by the closest things to risk-free investment—a government bond or a prime-rate bank loan. The size of allowed profit rates does not justify the use of regulation to protect regulated firms from uncertainty.

Continuity of service is also probably overvalued by regulators, particularly in such regulated industries as airline transportation or broadcasting. The issue raised by a new technology is rarely one of a threat to service, but of who should provide a service and how they should provide it. Occasionally a new technology promises gains for users of nearly all services from a particular industry, but cannot provide a particular service offered by the old mode. This circumstance can create a substantial problem for users of the particular service; however, the value of the particular service is not necessarily infinite, nor the priority of continuing it always absolute. The benefit of a new technology to other members of society may outweigh the losses to its users of discontinuing an old service.

Product and Process Quality Controls

All regulatory decisions are supposed to be based on the general consumer interests pertaining to the regulated industry. One class of regulatory responsibilities gives, in essence, a government seal of approval to products or services, providing either a guarantee of minimum quality or an assurance that a product or process will have an effect that is tolerable to members of society other than the consumers of the good or service. This type of activity is similar to franchising, except that it is not intended to be a vehicle for preventing competition.

As with franchising, many quality control responsibilities are lodged in agencies that the Ash Council did not examine, such as the Food and Drug Administration, the Federal Housing Administration, the Environmental Protection Agency, the Federal Aviation Administration, the Board of Governors of the Federal Reserve System, and several others. Among the regulatory agencies, the Securities and Exchange Commission and the Federal Trade Commission have important quality control responsibilities, the transportation agencies have some authority in regulating service safety, and all have responsibilities to protect the environment.

Quality control regulation has often been quite successful. In some industries regulated firms favor reasonably high performance standards, thus easing the job of regulators. For example, regulation has encouraged widespread acceptance of air travel, financial institutions, and corporate equities by reducing consumer risks. Other industries, although they may regard quality regulation as a nuisance and would prefer that it be eliminated, find that the cost of meeting regulatory standards is not very high. For example, the textile and fur labeling requirements enforced by the FTC probably fall in this category. In most cases the "Do Not Remove Under Penalty of Law" tags probably provide little benefit to consumers, but labeling is cheap. Here regulation creates a visible product and does no serious damage to anyone. Perhaps this is why the FTC is particularly tenacious in enforcing its textile and fur labeling rules; well over half of the complaints and cease-and-desist orders issued by the FTC in 1970 pertained to the regulation of material labels, and the fraction is growing.

Most quality control regulation is neither favored by industry nor inexpensive to comply with. In these cases the results are more controversial, and the proper extent of regulation more open to debate. Most of the alleged failings of regulation are of rules that have not been made and activities that regulators have chosen not to undertake. Such failures are difficult to prove and highly conjectural.

Nearly all of the controversial quality control regulation is done outside the independent regulatory commissions, and is therefore discussed in Chapter 5. The two exceptions are, first, the regulation of advertising by the FTC through its "deceptive practices" authority and by the FCC through its more general authority over broadcasting, and second, the environmental protection responsibilities of all regulatory agencies.

Regulatory agencies have only reluctantly considered environmental issues, despite laws, executive orders, and court decisions explicitly establishing the germaneness of these issues. For example, in January 1970, the FCC, in authorizing an FM station that would have constructed its transmitting tower in a National Seashore, explicitly refused to consider objections on environmental grounds from the National Park Service. Nine months later, after the prospective licensee had withdrawn his application, and after a Department of Interior petition had argued that the FCC had not obeyed legal mandates, the FCC rescinded its authorization.[13]

All regulatory agencies fall under the jurisdiction of executive orders requiring federal agencies to consider the environmental effects of agency decisions and policies, and the FPC is explicitly required by law to consider all aspects, including the effect on the environment, of prospective hydroelectric installations. Yet the agencies, when faced with deciding whether to consider the environmental issue, persistently have taken positions excessively favorable to industry, giving inadequate consideration to the general public problem surrounding questionable investments desired by regulated firms.

The pervasive argument against stricter enforcement of rules protecting consumers is that it would cause a sacrifice of employment, output, and consumption that is not warranted by the qualitative gains that strict regulation would produce. This argument is valid only with respect to a particular industry or activity. If each industry is required to make up for, or to prevent, the damage it does to others or to give honest information about the quality of its product, the result will be a redistribution of business among industries. Whether the public issue is pollution abatement, truth in advertising, product effectiveness, or product safety, the result of effective regulation is simply to raise the costs of the products and services of firms that rely more heavily on socially detrimental practices than do other firms. But this will not cause employment to decline generally. Federal government monetary, fiscal, retraining, and redevelopment policies are the appropriate means to ensure the maintenance of full employment. Strict enforcement is likely to cause a redistribution of employment and profits among firms, and it is this effect that concerns regulators.

13. F.C.C. 70-41 (20 FCC 2nd 988) and F.C.C. 70-1061 (25 FCC 2nd 877).

An Aside on Coordination

The Ash Council believes that policy coordination among regulatory agencies and between the agencies and other parts of government would confer important benefits. The lack of interagency coordination is a common complaint about regulation, particularly with respect to the transportation agencies. In the literature evaluating regulation widespread support would be found for most of the Ash report proposals for greater coordination. Nevertheless, the report does not discuss one important argument against coordination and in one case goes overboard in the amount of coordination it asserts is desirable.

The principal argument against coordination follows from the observation that regulation has become anticompetitive. In the sector in which coordination seems most obviously desirable—transportation—the opposition to coordination is also strongest, for the transportation agencies have been most active in preventing competition. The Ash Council recommends that the ICC, the CAB, and the Federal Maritime Commission be merged. But why should the merger of these agencies change their philosophy of regulation? Merging the agencies could mean removing the last vestiges of competition in transportation—air versus surface. Furthermore, the new agency most likely would be dominated by the oldest and largest agency, the ICC. The ICC does regulate all long-distance surface transport, and most experts agree that the "coordination" offered by single-agency regulation of surface transport has produced disastrous results.[14] The prospects of a new policy to direct the future growth of all transportation—surface and air—in the same way are certainly unattractive.

The Ash Council also recommends that the antitrust policies of the FTC be coordinated with the general economic policies of the administration. The connection between antitrust enforcement and general economic policy is tenuous at best; the report only asserts that coordination is needed. The proposal that the Council of Economic Advisers play a major policy role in the FTC is particularly difficult to support. Competitive policies are absolutes of government activity. Monopolistic abuses are presumably as bad in a depression as in an inflationary boom, in progressive as well as in static industries. The principal responsibilities of the CEA are to advise the President on policies to improve the performance of the national economy with respect to employ-

14. The Ash Council concurs in this view, chastising the ICC because it "overlooks the central consideration of which mode is best suited to carry the traffic." See *A New Regulatory Framework*, p. 71.

ment, growth, and price stability. The powers given the FTC to prevent and to penalize unfair business practices were not intended to be used in a discretionary way in connection with other objectives. In particular, suppose a President were to decide to reestablish a "jawbone" policy toward private wage and price decisions as an anti-inflation device; it would seem an especially bad idea to "coordinate" decisions to prosecute firms that are guilty of unfair business practices with attempts to influence business decisions about prices and wages.

Summary Evaluation of Regulation

The preceding discussion of regulatory failures only summarizes a vast literature in which regulators are accused of being excessively concerned about the welfare of the regulated. The Ash Council raises the issue only once, then quickly dismisses it as one of several effects, rather than a cause, of the deficiencies of regulation. According to the Council, "it would be easy to attribute dissatisfaction with the performance of regulatory commissions . . . to over-identification with the industries regulated. . . . In our view, however, these and other points of dissatisfaction are symptoms. The cause is more fundamental."[15] With a bit of nostalgia for old regulatory problems and apparently a belief that regulation was more effective in the past, the Council identifies the real problem as the inability of the organizational structure of regulation to cope with the growing demands placed upon it. Thus "the commissions, perhaps suitable to a simpler day, have not been freed from structural restraints that are antithetic to the accomplishment of their new missions."[16]

The complaints outlined above indicate that the problem of regulation runs far deeper than ineptitude by the agencies. According to the alternative view, the regulatory agencies, by attempting to maintain the status quo in regulated industries, are making policies that are not in the public interest. Consequently, the performance of regulated industries falls short of a reasonable, attainable social objective because the regulators have a different definition of the public interest than does society generally.

Certainly regulators do not choose their objectives irrespective of the influences operating on them; consequently organizational issues raised by the Ash Council are intimately related to the failings of regulation. But if the problem with regulation is the misspecification of objectives, rather than an inability

15. *Ibid.*, p. 31.
16. *Ibid.*, pp. 31-32.

to achieve generally acceptable objectives, the proper organizational arrangement for regulation is not necessarily the one suggested by the Ash Council.
In investigating this issue, a plausible political and organizational theory to
explain the misspecification of goals by an agency and a broader array of
empirical information than the facts considered by the Ash Council are needed.
The numerous regulatory agencies within the federal government include
examples of almost every organizational form. If the empirical base is spread
wider still to capture the variety in state and local government regulatory
agencies, a considerable body of information exists for examining the relative
effectiveness of alternative organizational structures.

CHAPTER FOUR

THEORIES OF REGULATION

Of all the topics relating to regulation, certainly regulatory theory has been least studied. A "theory of regulation" would offer a plausible explanation of why regulatory agencies behave as they do. Its elements would include propositions about the motivation of regulators, about interactions between the regulatory environment and the regulators' choices of policy goals and instruments, and about the relationship of regulation to the political system.

The Traditional View of Regulation

As others have observed, independent regulatory commissions were not established according to a well conceived theory.[1] In fact, the most important characteristics of regulatory agencies—independence and a judicial atmosphere —came about largely by accident. The first commission—the Interstate Commerce Commission (ICC)—was originally part of the Department of the Interior; however, friction between the senator who guided the legislation establishing the ICC and the Harrison administration, combined with the desire of the secretary of the interior to avoid responsibility for the ICC, led to its redefinition as an independent agency. The ICC's first chairman, a respected jurist, was responsible for establishing the formal procedures of the ICC, and the Congress did not attempt to interfere.

Despite this rather haphazard beginning, most analysts believe that the independent regulatory agency was the creature of several pervasive and rather naive political attitudes running deep in American society. First is the general distrust of the political system coupled with a faith in nonpolitical expert judgments. Politicians are held to be easily corruptible and consequently are not to be trusted with important decisions about business behavior. Instead,

1. For a more complete treatment, see Marver H. Bernstein, *Regulating Business by Independent Commission* (Princeton University Press, 1955).

these decisions should be left to experts insulated from the corrupt politicians. Second is the belief that most Americans are in general agreement about social policy. According to this belief, Americans are relatively homogeneous. Consequently, a uniform, consistent "best" public policy exists, and is both recognizable and feasible. Third, government interference in private decisions should be minimized. Only in exceptional circumstances is intervention required, and even in these cases the principal objective of government action should be to save capitalistic, free enterprise institutions from destroying themselves through their own abuses, rather than radically to alter the institutions creating social problems. In sum, society needs governmental agencies to protect it from two atypical members: the occasional unethical businessman (originally a monopolist, but with the onset of the Great Depression a free-wheeling competitor also became suspect) and the corrupt politician who could be bribed to protect the former's abuses from social reform.

Independent commissions, composed of nonpolitical men who were beholden neither to the politicians nor to the businessmen committing the abuses requiring regulation, would be unsusceptible to political corruption. By specializing for several years, perhaps throughout their careers, in a particular problem of business behavior, the members would become expert enough to detect the socially most desirable policy. In a homogeneous society, only a handful of unethical people would formulate unacceptable policies, and independence would guard against that result.

According to the traditional view, regulation could fail either if independence were lost or if the authority of the agency were not sharply limited. Both sources of failure are frequently cited as the principal causes of regulatory problems.

The Independence of Independent Agencies

Many former commissioners and academic experts agree that in no meaningful sense is regulation independent, especially of the Congress. Like other government agencies, independent regulatory commissions need annual congressional appropriations as well as legislative authority to alter the scope of their responsibility. This gives the Congress enormous leverage over general agency policy and even over individual decisions. In fact, as former Securities and Exchange Commission (SEC) Chairman William L. Cary has pointed out, it gives substantial leverage not to the Congress in general, but to specific individuals and subcommittees within the Congress.[2] Congressmen try to

2. William L. Cary, *Politics and the Regulatory Agencies* (McGraw-Hill, 1967). See especially p. 57.

influence all kinds of agency activities, including staffing, policy making, and decisions on specific cases. According to Cary, "it is safe to conclude that agencies seldom take controversial steps under their rule making power which do not have some support from Congress. In view of his almost autocratic powers, the [congressional] committee chairman's views are likely to be given extraordinary weight."[3]

One tactic of the congressional committee is to hold hearings on a case pending before a regulatory commission. In one of the several cases cited by Cary—The Pillsbury Company v. Federal Trade Commission—the courts threw out the FTC decision on the grounds that a hearing by the Senate Subcommittee on Antitrust and Monopoly, held concurrently with the FTC investigation, put substantial pressure on the FTC that could have affected the agency's decision.[4] Seymour Scher, after investigating the attitudes of congressmen toward interfering with the National Labor Relations Board, concluded that "the Committee member recognizes no limitations on his behavior by virtue of the agency's judicial functions." Of the ten members of the House Labor Committee interviewed by Scher, nine expressed the view that the NLRB was "political" and that pressuring the agency was legitimate. One congressman remarked, "We never think twice about calling the Board and asking for a little special handling of some cases."[5]

The independent status of the regulatory agencies may even exacerbate the problem of nonstatutory congressional intervention. Because the agency does not have the political protection of the President or a cabinet official, congressmen have little fear of political reprisal when dealing with an independent agency. Since commissioners acting alone have far less public stature than do high-level administration officials, independence serves primarily to insulate the agency from the general public; the agency has no effective means of appealing for popular support in a conflict with a congressional committee. The problem is aggravated by the relative decline in the importance of regulatory agencies, which has made it even more difficult for the agency to capture public attention.[6]

There is less agreement that the President exercises effective control over agency activities. In principle, the President has a number of powers that

3. *Ibid.*, p. 53.
4. *Ibid.*, p. 56.
5. Seymour Scher, "Congressional Committee Members as Independent Agency Overseers: A Case Study," *American Political Science Review,* Vol. 54 (December 1960), pp. 911-20. The quotations are from pp. 920 and 919, respectively.
6. For a complete discussion of the points made here, see Bernstein, *Regulating Business by Independent Commission.*

could be used to influence agencies. First is through the role that the Office of Management and Budget plays in overseeing the budget and the legislative programs of all federal agencies. Second is the power of the President to appoint the chairmen of all agencies except the ICC, an authority dating from 1950 and made more important in the early sixties, when the powers of several chairmen were expanded. Third, given the pattern of expirations of appointments to commissions, the President appoints a majority to each commission within three to eight years (or less if some commissioners resign before their terms are over, as frequently happens). Fourth is the limited legislative power that inheres in the authority to issue executive orders on matters of legally established government policy, as is exemplified by the 1970 order that regulatory agencies, among other government bureaus, give full standing to the issue of environmental management in deliberations about agency policy.[7] In addition, the President has a number of specific responsibilities written into various regulatory laws, such as the right to approve or reject international airline route awards by the Civil Aeronautics Board (CAB) or orders from the SEC to suspend trading.

Although the President could exercise authority over regulatory agencies, there is little evidence that he or his administration makes much of an attempt to do so. A report by the Bureau of the Budget in 1950 contended that the budgeting process is extremely cursory and has little effect with respect to independent regulatory agencies, partly because there is little interest in the agencies and partly because the budgets are so small.[8] No one contends that the 1950 assessment has become substantially less valid twenty years later. Occasionally an appointment to an agency or a new regulatory issue causes a flurry of interest in the agency on the part of the Executive Office, but this is unusual and short-lived. Even rare improprieties by presidential officials appear half-hearted and inept, as in the famous Adams-Goldfine case during the Eisenhower years.[9]

Cary explains the President's general lack of interest in regulatory matters on the grounds that there is little political gain to be made from paying close attention to regulation. "As a practical matter, even excellent administration of the commissions will probably not help the President much politically."[10] Only a scandal or some other regulatory question that captures widespread publicity, says Cary, can cause the White House to become interested.

7. National Environmental Policy Act of 1969, P.L. 91-190, Jan. 1, 1970.
8. U.S. Bureau of the Budget, "Project Summary, Survey of Regulatory Commissions" (1950; processed); cited in Bernstein, *Regulating Business by Independent Commission*, p. 144.
9. See Cary, *Politics and the Regulatory Agencies*, pp. 13 ff. for a discussion of Sherman Adams's attempt to influence regulatory decisions.
10. *Ibid.*, p. 8.

Since Presidents do not appear disposed to use the authority that they already have over regulatory agencies, it is difficult to imagine how incorporating regulatory agencies in the executive branch, as proposed by the Ash Council, would significantly increase presidential interest in regulation. All of the present motivations to ignore regulatory issues would remain. The shield of presidential political power will protect the agencies against the budget cutter's axe and attempted coercion by the Congress only if the President actively makes the shield available. While the Ash Council has proposed the only possible plan for transferring the political power of the President to the regulatory agencies, it is debatable whether even this would be effective; if not, the nation may have to face accommodating business policy to incurably defective regulatory agencies. One source of information on the likely success of the Ash Council proposal is the willingness of the President to defend the regulatory agencies that are already inside the cabinet structure. This will be discussed in Chapter 5.

The Nature of the Regulatory Mandate

Several observers have pointed out that the nature of the mandate to regulatory agencies was profoundly altered by the Transportation Act of 1920.[11] Prior to 1920, regulation was oriented toward preventing the abuses of monopoly. The Interstate Commerce Act of 1887, the Sherman Antitrust Act of 1890, and the Clayton and the Federal Trade Commission Acts of 1914 had all given government agencies a mandate to attack specific problems associated with concentrated economic power. In addition, these acts had, more or less, tried to specify the types of behavior that were to be regarded as antisocial, giving enforcement officials a reasonably clear idea of what they were supposed to prevent.

The Transportation Act of 1920 was the first of a series of laws passed over the course of two decades that embodied an entirely new type of mandate. First, the laws were often distinctly anticompetition rather than antimonopoly. The power to set minimum rates and the duty to oversee the orderly development of an industry—the principal additions of the 1920 act to the ICC's responsibilities—have a distinctly different philosophy than did the maximum-rate regulation and the clear prohibition against the short-haul, long-haul rate differentials which were established in 1887. Second, the delegation of responsibility to the regulatory agency ceased being specific. No

11. This section is an amalgam of the ideas set forth in Bernstein, *Regulating Business by Independent Commission;* Henry J. Friendly, *The Federal Administrative Agencies: The Need for Newer Definitions of Standards* (Harvard University Press, 1962); and Theodore Lowi, *The End of Liberalism: Ideology, Policy, and the Crisis of Public Authority* (Norton, 1969).

longer was the mandate simply to prevent certain reasonably well understood (if not well defined) practices. Agencies were now given very general, unspecified authority to manage an industry in the "public interest." The thrust of these two additions to the responsibilities of regulation was to make regulatory agencies a form of legal cartel for the regulated firms. Activities that would be clear violations of antitrust statutes if practiced by trade associations or informal meetings of industry executives were permitted and even condoned if overseen by regulators. A recent example is the negotiation of a joint reduction in the number of transcontinental flights by the major trunk air carriers. The CAB promoted this obvious example of cartel behavior.

The "new regulation" replaced the rule of law with uncertainty and continual bargaining over the bounds of legitimate behavior. Policy issues were to be decided in the same manner as lawsuits, through adversary arguments before a tribunal. Yet in regulation there is no counterpart to the criminal statutes that define socially unacceptable behavior. Instead, behavioral rules—as well as decisions whether specific acts are in violation of the rules—are determined through the adversary-judicial process. In short, according to Lowi, "modern law has become a series of instructions to administrators rather than a series of commands to citizens."[12] Consequently it is little wonder that, through time, regulatory decisions seem inconsistent and mutually contradictory, without a legitimate basis in the underlying economic realities of the regulated industry. Different cases dealing with the same issues are argued with unequal persuasiveness on all sides of the dispute; precedent is unimportant since no rules are binding; each new appointee to a commission is free to make his own interpretation of the public interest.

A number of defects of regulation are related to the vagueness of the regulatory mandate: unequal treatment of like cases, additional uncertainty introduced by regulatory inconsistency, elaborate legal procedures since each case is essentially a new law, and a much heavier case load since a past adverse decision does not adequately deter raising an issue again.

The Ash Council recognizes the problem of vagueness in regulatory policy, but interprets it in a quite different way. The problem as seen by the Council is not bad legislation, but the inability of an independent, collegial body to agree on general policy pronouncements. The Council contends that a single administrator, protected politically by the President, would have the time and political courage to make policy, particularly if his rights of review of staff decisions were reduced: first, by imposing a time limit; second, by limiting the issues of internal review to whether a decision is consistent with

12. Lowi, *The End of Liberalism,* p. 144.

agency policy; third, by requiring explicit policy explanations when decisions are remanded.

The Ash Council did not propose changes in the broad discretionary powers of regulatory agencies. Even if the Council's proposals were adopted, policy could still take wide swings, without legislative mandate, as administrations and even administrators changed. Furthermore, since swings in policy would probably be wider with a single administrator than with a collegial body, the uncertainties and inconsistencies of regulation would be likely to increase.

Summary: Traditional Theory, Independence, and Vagueness

One need not hold to the traditional view of regulation—that a truly autonomous body with a limited, explicit mandate is the most effective regulatory institution—to believe that the central problems with regulation are undesirable congressional interference and the lack of a clear legislative mandate. Nevertheless, these beliefs are consistent with the traditional view of regulation and are the arguments usually cited by individuals who subscribe, more or less, to the traditional theory.

Neither problem necessarily undermines the proposals in the Ash report. Independence from the Congress might be purchasable only through bringing regulation under the influence (and political protection) of the President; the independent, collegial form might be ineffective in enforcing clear, as well as fuzzy, laws. Yet the Ash report does not explicitly make either claim, for it does not deal directly with either issue. Perhaps the choice was politic. Criticizing the Congress for putting unethical pressure on agencies and for enacting bad legislation is probably not the most effective tactic to induce the Congress to make reforms. Nevertheless, the issues are highly important to the problem of designing an effective, socially responsive regulatory institution, for there is justification for the view that the Ash Council proposals will not substantially ameliorate either of these problems.

The Political Economics of Regulation

The traditional theory of regulation is based on the view that the regulatory process is efficient and perfectible. According to this view, regulatory ineffectiveness arises from various externally imposed difficulties, such as coercion by politicians, improper structure of the agency, a bad legislative mandate, or inadequate means for obtaining information, general political support, and coordination with other agencies.

An alternative view is that inherent in the regulatory process is a persistent tendency to make socially undesirable policy, even if the agency is motivated to "do good" rather than to promote the regulated industry. The most developed theory of regulation having this characteristic is an extension of the more general marriage of political science and economics, called political economics or social choice. A fundamental assumption of political economics is that many types of political behavior can be explained and predicted on the basis of their effects on the distribution of income and wealth. Since regulation deals with questions relating to the distribution of wealth almost to the exclusion of other issues, it is an obvious arena for the political economist.[13]

Performance Criteria and Mobilization of Bias

Even if regulators seek to strike the proper balance between general public welfare and the interests of a specific group, and even if they are rational in pursuing this objective, they still must find observable success indicators. For a private enterprise, the success indicator normally is after-tax profits, or perhaps sales or the trend in earnings per share; to a law office, it can be cases won and the size of judgments; to a politician, it is reelection. To a regulatory authority, one success indicator is a negative one—the failure of the courts or the Congress to override a decision by the regulators, on either procedural or substantive grounds. A second success indicator is continued operation of the regulated sector. Widespread service failure is likely to be blamed on the regulatory agency, and is therefore to be avoided, even if the cost exceeds the costs of the service failure.

Because regulatory agencies are relatively small and generally out of the limelight, they can normally expect to be ignored by the political system. The agency's performance might be made a political issue if a series of its decisions aroused the wrath of a particular group. In order for a group to decide to carry a battle with a regulatory agency to either the courts or the political arena, the group must expect a substantial gain if the regulatory decision is overturned. Appealing the decision of an agency, either legally or politically, is expensive. To an organized group, costs are incurred through effectively lobbying the politicians or fighting a court case. To an unorganized

13. The analysis in this section is based on points raised by Bernstein, *Regulating Business by Independent Commission;* James M. Buchanan and Gordon Tullock, *The Calculus of Consent: Logical Foundations of Constitutional Democracy* (University of Michigan Press, 1962); Lance E. Davis and Douglass C. North, *Institutional Change and American Economic Growth* (Cambridge University Press, 1971); Anthony Downs, *An Economic Theory of Democracy* (Harper, 1957), and *Inside Bureaucracy* (Little Brown, 1967); William H. Riker, *The Theory of Political Coalition* (Yale University Press, 1962); and Roger G. Noll, "The Behavior of Regulatory Agencies," *Review of Social Economy,* Vol. 29 (March 1971), pp. 15-19.

group, the costs are even higher, for the group must become organized to be effective. The expected gain must exceed these battle costs to induce "mobilization of a bias" in order to mount an appeal.

Most regulatory issues are of deep interest to regulated industries, with a very substantial amount of income for these industries riding on the decision. The stake of the general public may in the aggregate be even higher, but it is diffused among a large number of unorganized individuals. Issues of regulation are likely to be extremely important to the welfare of the individuals in a regulated industry; however, to society at large any given regulatory issue is likely to be far down the list of concerns. The motivation of a single firm to fight an unfavorable regulatory decision is very high, while a regulatory decision unfavorable to the general public is unlikely to generate enough interest to cause a general public issue to be raised. This explains Herring's observation on the atmosphere in which regulatory agencies operate: "The milieu is distinctly one of special interests. . . . The commission performs its duties in surroundings far from neutral. . . ."[14]

An agency that tries to minimize the chance of being overruled by subsequent legal or legislative decisions must, when the interests of a regulated firm and its customers or the public generally are at odds, be overly responsive to the interests of the regulated.[15] First, by giving regulated firms a little more than they deserve, the agencies make certain that the most threatening group has something that could be lost in an appeal. In disputes between well-represented interests, the agency will, for the same reason, seek a compromise that gives something to all disputants, whether economic efficiency or the public interest would favor such a compromise. Second, the regulatory agency will want to be sure that it cannot legitimately be accused of being unfair to the groups that are most likely to challenge the decision. Furthermore, agency determinations of "fact" are bound to be based on evidence supplied by the represented special interests. Most of the information flowing to the agency will come from the regulated, who can afford to use much better resources in regulatory cases than will be employed to represent the interests of the general public.

To protect itself from charges of neglecting an interest to a dispute, the agency can develop elaborate information-gathering and decision-making pro-

14. E. Pendleton Herring, *Public Administration and the Public Interest* (McGraw-Hill, 1936), pp. 183 and 194.

15. The importance of this tendency, of course, varies among agencies according to the stake of the general public in the agency's responsibilities and the extent of conflict between the regulated industry and the general public interest. For example, there is not likely to be a substantial public interest in most of the disputes between business and labor adjudicated before the NLRB.

cedures. These also serve to raise the costs of entering a regulatory dispute, making participation in a policy issue by groups other than the regulated firms even less likely.

Another safety device is to exercise extreme caution in approving new technologies and service innovations, particularly if they threaten to redistribute income within the regulated sector or between the regulated sector and the general public. The Federal Communications Commission's position, somewhat loosened in 1968, on the "foreign attachment" prohibition is a case in point. The claim that telephones made by someone other than Western Electric would seriously undermine the performance of the entire telephone network, while far-fetched, just might have been correct (the threat of cataclysmic failure), and, after all, how many people would want to make a federal case out of being denied an exotic telephone? With new technology come many uncertainties about performance, financial success, and the welfare of related firms and industries. The effects of old technology are much more easily calculated. Thus, when an issue involves new technology, the chance of making a decision that disturbs the existing distribution of income and provision of services is high; the rational agency response is to postpone the decision until more information is available or, if possible, to transfer the responsibility for making the decision to someone else. When a decision must be faced, the agency tends to try to spread the risks and benefits of the innovation among as many parties to the dispute as possible.

If an agency evenhandedly balances the interests of society generally against the interests of the regulated, it will continually find itself called upon to defend its decisions before the courts and the Congress. Yet when it shows some degree of favoritism to the regulated, the response of these public institutions leads it to believe quite wrongly that its decisions are satisfactory. Thus the agency can very well believe it is behaving in the public interest simply because the institutions that can reverse the agency are not being called upon—at least not effectively—to do so. But this is a result not of evenhandedness on the part of the agency, but of the great difficulty the general public has in making known its dissatisfaction. As Cary said, because there is little political gain in effective regulation, ineffective regulation will result— for there *is* political gain (votes and campaign contributions from individuals associated with the regulated industries) to be had there.

The Nature of Commissioners

The tendency of the legal-political system to reinforce a proindustry bias in regulatory agencies could well be magnified by the process by which commission members are chosen. Most appointees are politicians with a background in law. Commissioners with this background are likely to place greater weight on legal and political feedback than would, say, economists or academic lawyers, who are more likely to consider efficiency and equity.

In theory, regulatory commissions are composed of neutral, objective experts on the affairs of the regulated industry and on the public interest in the behavior of the regulated. In practice, appointees to commissions must have the tacit approval of the regulated industries. Appointments, almost unnoticed by the general public, are closely watched by regulated firms.[16] Rarely does the President appoint, and the Senate confirm, a commissioner if the regulated industry is politically aligned against him. While the appointment process does not necessarily produce commissioners who are consciously controlled by the industry they regulate, it nearly always succeeds in excluding persons who are regarded as opposed to the interests of the regulated. Of course, sometimes a maverick is appointed, largely because his behavior as a commissioner cannot be perfectly predicted. Nevertheless, unpredictable appointees are an exception, so that the distribution of views on commissions is likely to be less representative of views contrary to regulated interests than the distribution in society generally.

Proposals to appoint better commissioners, without altering the structure and responsibilities of the commission, can never really solve this problem. While it is conceivable that a campaign to induce the President to appoint more able commissioners could succeed, it is less likely that the appointment process—even if more expert persons can be found—will ever be immune to pressures from the regulated industry. The best that can be hoped for under the present arrangement is a commissioner who begins his term without fixed views on regulatory matters, and who has a receptive but neutral attitude toward the regulated firms. Even if such a person is appointed, the environment of regulatory agencies is likely to cause him to become sympathetic to the regulated as he gains experience.

Because of the limited range of views represented on commissions, regulatory policy is likely to be biased in favor of the regulated interests.[17] Policies of multiheaded bodies such as regulatory commissions tend to be at the median position within the group. The middle-of-the-road individual can always lead a majority against any proposal that he opposes. For example, suppose

16. This problem is obviously exacerbated by having a multimember body rather than a single administrator.

17. Conflicting, powerful regulated interests will both succeed in limiting the extent to which a commissioner can be biased against them, in addition to placing other restrictions on the points of view permitted on the commission.

that among five CAB members, the opinions about the "right" fare increase for trunk airlines are 1, 2, 3, 4, and 5 percent. If one commissioner proposes 4 percent, then the advocate of 3 percent can convince two other commissioners to vote against the 4 percent proposal by offering to propose 3 percent after 4 percent has been defeated.

Because the appointment process distorts the distribution of views on commissions, the median position on issues in which general and special interests are in conflict will lie somewhere between the unabashed proindustry view and the middle ground. The result will be a policy decision excessively responsive to the industry, although short of the policy an industry cartel—interested only in industry welfare—would have chosen.

The median-position rule is not always valid in units responsible for several different areas of public policy. Then each member of the body acts not only on the basis of his most desired position on each issue but also on his assessment of the sacrifice he is willing to make on one issue to gain his most desired position on another. In the CAB example, the agency might also be considering a change in policy on food and drink service. On the issue of how many alcoholic beverages a passenger shall be permitted to purchase, the median position may be two; however, a commissioner favoring a two-drink maximum may be willing to raise the maximum to three if in return he can get one more percentage point in the allowed price increase. If the member favoring a 3 percent price increase is willing to add 1 percent to the price increase in order to raise the drink limit to three, the final decision might be to allow three drinks and a 4 percent price increase—neither being the median position on the specific issues.

The possibility of vote trading is a good argument in favor of commissions as opposed to single administrators. Unfortunately, regulatory agencies, as special-purpose policy-making bodies, have little opportunity to effect such trade-offs among interest groups. As a result, no matter how intense his views, a commissioner outside the median position can have little effect on a policy outcome, particularly if the interest he represents has not been mobilized to lobby its position or to appeal an unfavorable decision. In a general-purpose policy-making body, such as a legislature, a member with a very strong interest in a particular issue has much more opportunity to consummate a vote-trading arrangement.

The preceding analysis leads to the conclusion that the policy-making authority of regulators should be limited as much as possible, leaving them primarily concerned with administrative matters and specific case decisions. Giving a special-purpose body broad policy-making power creates a situation which eliminates the possibility of mutually beneficial vote trading on unrelated policy matters.

Conclusions

According to the political economics view, it is not surprising that regulation has evolved from the antimonopoly zealotry of the turn-of-the-century agencies to the cartel-like behavior of today. Once the worst abuses of monopoly were abated (the short-haul, long-haul rate differentials and the trust-building of the robber barons), the public interest in regulation also declined. The main parties at interest before regulatory agencies—and the main political threats to the agencies—became the regulated industries. As long as an agency can prevent similar gross abuses from recurring, it is relatively safe from reprisal through a grass-roots political movement.

While the political economics view of regulation predicts continuing public dissatisfaction with regulatory agencies, it shares the position of the traditional theory on the question of how specific regulatory laws should be. Regulation is usually established when public interest in some specific type of business behavior is at its peak. It is important that the regulatory agency be limited by law to dealing with the issue that caused public concern, and that new public concerns lead to new, specific mandates to regulators. While regulatory policy should be responsive to a changing social environment, Congress as the more representative body should institute the changes. If the regulatory mandate is broad, in time some of the social gains of the regulatory process will be squandered in attempts to protect (typically from competition) the regulated industry.

Nothing in the political economics view justifies the belief that regulation will be substantially more or less effective if it is inside the executive branch. A legitimate test of this view is whether moving an agency from independent status into the executive branch changes the behavior of the agency. The political economics view does not consider the structure of the agency important (whether the agency is collegial or headed by a single administrator) in determining its ability to arrive at decisions that are in the public interest, except insofar as commissions offer some opportunity for vote trading. While not necessarily inconsistent with the Ash Council's arguments about delays and inefficiencies resulting from a collegial form, the political economics view predicts that a substantial amount of the inefficiency of an agency is intentional—serving to raise the costs of fighting regulatory battles and to minimize uncertainties about the effects of decisions. According to this view, regulatory agencies headed by a single administrator and located under the wing of the

President will still be agonizingly slow in making important decisions and will still adopt highly formalistic procedures.

The political economics approach obviously does not explain all regulatory behavior or all the influences acting on regulators. The general public interest is sometimes effectively represented in regulatory matters, despite the institutional barriers. The mass media often champion a cause solely on equity or moral grounds, and some crusaders are willing to make personal sacrifices to publicize and muster political support for general interest groups, such as consumers. Political economic theory has no satisfactory explanation for this behavior, nor can it predict which policy issues will capture public attention through the efforts of volunteers who advance ethical arguments. But the public conscience cannot be devoted to an infinity of public policy issues simultaneously. Most issues are bound to be largely invisible for long periods of time. It is here that political economic theory is most appropriate.

CHAPTER FIVE

SOME SPECIFIC REGULATORY ARENAS

In this chapter selected regulatory activities are examined to determine the nature of the problems surrounding them. Two of the agencies examined are discussed in the Ash report—the Federal Power Commission (FPC) and the Federal Trade Commission (FTC). The latter is compared with an agency having a similar function—the Antitrust division of the Department of Justice. The remaining discussion focuses on regulatory activities involving several agencies that were not examined by the Council, but which have interesting characteristics that provide some insight into the effect on performance of organizational structure and other factors. The agencies discussed are the National Labor Relations Board (NLRB—an independent commission that was not examined in the Ash report), the Tariff Commission (an independent commission serving a purely policy advisory function), the Oil Import Appeals Board (OIA—a commission inside a cabinet department), the Food and Drug Administration (FDA—a regulatory agency with a single administrator inside a cabinet department), the various agencies regulating banking (agencies that share a responsibility that raises coordination problems), and the agencies with regulatory functions in the Department of Agriculture.

The discussion that follows illustrates three important aspects of regulation. (1) The extent of regulatory activities is enormous. (2) There is significant variety in the organizational structure of regulation, as well as in the type of mandates that have been given to regulators. (3) Regardless of the organizational form, most regulatory agencies are subject to the same type of criticism as the independent collegial bodies examined by the Ash Council.

The National Labor Relations Board

The most important independent regulatory agency not examined in the Ash report is the National Labor Relations Board, which is in charge of overseeing collective bargaining in order to protect the rights of workers and employers. The NLRB, as was indicated in Chapter 4, is subjected to a substantial amount of congressional pressure, because of its responsibility to investigate charges of unfair labor practices against specific employers or unions. Congressmen who feel strongly about cases involving their constituents are, as Scher argues, not averse to expressing themselves directly to the Board.[1]

The NLRB's environment would at first glance appear to be especially receptive to case-by-case decisions, without any coherent and overriding policy. The NLRB would thus have enough freedom in deciding each case to accommodate the pressures placed on it from the outside. Precisely the opposite is true; as Friendly has pointed out, the NLRB "has done much to translate the general words of its charter into more specific guides for behavior by the regulated and decision by the regulators."[2] The agency's decisions often contain general discussions of the policy implications of the cases at hand, and the agency's annual report contains a section discussing the development of agency policy during the year.

The willingness of this independent commission, a collegial body subject to considerable congressional interference and without political protection from the White House, to make clear policy pronouncements is at variance with the general view of regulation propounded in the Ash report. Furthermore, as Friendly, a proponent of more specific regulatory mandates, has pointed out, the legislation that created the NLRB is characteristically vague. In many instances the Board has no coherent legislative guide as to what constitutes an unfair labor practice. Nevertheless, it has devoted much of its effort to clarifying the ground rules for collective bargaining, often sufficiently vexing the Congress to induce it to enact new laws in order to overturn NLRB policy. Most analysts would agree that this is how regulation ought to operate; but agencies where the policy-making aspect of regulation appears to work approximately as it should are a rarity. Two factors seem to be responsible for the NLRB's unusual performance.

The NLRB as Arbitrator between Strong Interests

The NLRB normally deals with two strong, effectively represented groups with conflicting economic interests. It cannot easily avoid antagonizing at least one side in a dispute and can expect a very large fraction of its decisions

1. See p. 35 above.
2. Henry J. Friendly, *The Federal Administrative Agencies: The Need for Better Definition of Standards* (Harvard University Press, 1962), p. 36.

to be appealed either politically or legally.[3] All of the attention of the NLRB to avoiding chastisement and reversal is therefore rationally directed toward reaching a decision that has the best chance of standing up in court. In addition to following correct legal procedures, the NLRB can increase the chance that its decisions will be upheld by making each decision appear to be one of a long series of similar decisions on similar issues. Coherent policy makes it easier to relate a current (contested) decision to past actions that the courts have not overturned. Furthermore, an historical policy that has not been overturned by legislation as a result of past decisions is unlikely to cause a congressional reaction in its latest reincarnation.

Other agencies, by contrast, normally deal with only one party to an issue—the regulated firm—seeking to change a price or a service. These agencies have less motivation to develop consistent policy because they have a far greater chance of avoiding the appeal by assuring that the strong party to a dispute captures some gain at the expense of the weak. The treatment of cases relating to similar issues can be quite different, as the relative strengths of the parties at interest vary from case to case. The gains and losses to be distributed by a particular decision are altered by the regulators according to the strengths of the disputants.

Other agencies do, of course, in some important instances adjudicate disputes among regulated interests. Route awards in transportation regulation; contested broadcast licenses and disputes between airwaves broadcasters and cable interests in communications; and the conflict between producers and retailers in gas field-price regulation are some examples. Nevertheless, few share all of the following important characteristics of NLRB cases: (1) Almost all NLRB cases are "zero sum" situations in which the losses of the loser will be as large as the gains of the winner. In most route award cases, for example, the issue is how to divide the growth in the demand for service: some will gain by the decision, but rarely will anyone lose. (2) The parties to NLRB disputes rarely find themselves in continual, long-term contact with the agency on numerous issues. Many cases are between a firm and a local union chapter over labor relations at a single plant. Other agencies usually deal with the same individuals in a large number of cases and are able to balance the favorable and unfavorable decisions pertaining to a particular interest. (3) While

3. Douglass V. Brown reports that currently about 60 percent of NLRB decisions are appealed to the federal courts, accounting for about half of *all* appeals of decisions of federal boards and commissions. See his presidential address, "Legalism and Industrial Relations in the United States," delivered at the annual meetings of the Industrial Relations Research Association, Detroit, December 1970 (Sloan School of Industrial Management, Massachusetts Institute of Technology; processed).

labor-management disputes certainly have some effect on the general public welfare, the interest of nondisputants is rarely as high as it is in cases before other regulatory agencies. The prime concern of the FCC in regulating the development of cable television, for instance, is to give cable interests enough leeway to allow cable development to be profitable, but not enough to cause cable to threaten the profits of over-the-air broadcasters, The welfare of the viewer is given much less attention. On August 5, 1971, in a letter to the relevant congressional subcommittees, the FCC stated that "our objective throughout has been to find a way of opening up cable's potential to serve the public without at the same time undermining the foundation of the existing . . . broadcast structure. . . . It would appear that the *minimum* number of distant signals that might reasonably open the way for cable development is two additional signals not available in the community. We will therefore permit this amount in the larger markets where it is necessary and feasible in terms of impact on broadcasting."[4] In rail route abandonment cases the ICC normally weighs the interests of the community threatened with loss of service against the railroad's interest in giving up a losing route. Not represented are the users of other rail services, who pay higher fares if a losing route is not abandoned.[5]

The NLRB as Referee, Not Conflict Resolver

The type of behavior the NLRB regulates also affects its performance. The Board does not impose administrative decisions in an arena where a simpler decision-making process is available, namely market competition. Other regulatory agencies are constantly seeking excuses for overriding the allocation of resources that a market would determine, an immensely difficult task even when it is justified. The NLRB does not make decisions in lieu of a market; rather it defines the rules that the parties to a dispute must abide by and determines what constitutes fair behavior by each party.[6] If the NLRB were like other agencies, it would be required to decide the terms of the final bargain between labor and management. For example, the Civil Aeronautics Board (CAB) not only is responsible for defining the issues relevant to a decision as to which airline will be awarded a particular route, but is also responsible for applying those criteria to the issue at hand and actually awarding the route.

4. FCC 71-787 63303. Emphasis added.
5. Merton J. Peck provided this excellent example.
6. Antitrust enforcement and securities regulation are similar to the NLRB's function, but neither normally requires adjudication of a conflict between two powerful interests in a situation in which little or no general public interest is at stake.

The NLRB does not specifically give away wealth to a successful party. Instead, it defines the rules under which conflicting parties must make their own decisions to divide wealth. While NLRB decisions obviously affect the terms of a final agreement, the agency does not determine what the final agreement should be. Instead, it bases its decisions on principles of democratic representation, the integrity of contracts, bargaining ethics, and other such concepts. These lend themselves to general policy making far more than purely economic matters which have less ethical content.

The Problem of Cumbersome Procedures

The NLRB is not free from criticism. The charge most often levied against it, aside from complaints about its legislative mandates (such as the Landrum-Griffin act),[7] is that it is excessively legalistic and formal. According to Douglass Brown, excessive legalism means two things—equating moral behavior with obedience to a set of rules and regulations, and an addiction among disputing parties to having someone else settle their problems.[8] The first leads to an ever-longer, more complex, and increasingly inflexible set of behavioral rules, making the job of engaging in and adjudicating collective bargaining increasingly difficult, cumbersome, time-consuming, and expensive. The second transfers some of the costs of collective bargaining to the public and, because the parties become less capable of deciding things for themselves, increases the proportion of bargaining issues that must be resolved by public intervention.

Brown's arguments are quite similar to the case made against other regulatory agencies—not only that regulation becomes increasingly cumbersome, but also that it tends to reduce the managerial effectiveness of the regulated firms. The regulatory agency, because it must ratify major business decisions and because it will try to protect the regulated firm from financial disaster, is said to weaken the quality of decision making by the regulated.

The legalism of the NLRB persists despite the fact that the agency has one organizational rule that the Ash Council argues ought to be adopted elsewhere. The Board itself does not have to make a formal decision in every case; after twenty days the decision of a trial examiner automatically becomes effective.[9] The persistence of legalism in the NLRB, despite limited review and a willingness to make policy, is evidence that one important cause of legalism is the importance attached to administrative procedures by the courts. Agencies can

7. Labor-Management Reporting and Disclosure Act of 1959, 73 Stat. 519.
8. *Ibid.,* p. 1.
9. National Labor Relations Act, amendments of 1947 to Sec. 10(C) (61 Stat. 137).

be expected to conclude that if their own procedures resemble court procedures more closely, the courts will be less likely to find them flawed. Especially in an agency like the NLRB that can expect such a high fraction of its decisions to be taken to the courts, the motivation for adopting elaborate procedures as a defense mechanism for agency decisions is very high.

The Food and Drug Administration

In many respects the Food and Drug Administration (FDA) is an example of the organizational structure of a regulatory agency that the Ash Council prefers. The FDA is run by a single administrator, and it is under the control of the President within the executive branch. The secretary of health, education, and welfare is legally responsible for the agency's activities. The principal difference between the FDA and the proposed structure for independent commissions is that the FDA is within a cabinet department, rather than being an office reporting directly to the President. Consequently, the FDA does not provide completely convincing evidence about the likely performance of agencies that are organized in the manner suggested by the Ash Council. Nevertheless, if having a single administrator who is formally a part of the President's administration has an important effect on the behavior of the agency, the performance of the FDA should reflect it.

Drug Regulation

The FDA has two responsibilities in drug regulation. The first, authorized under the Federal Food, Drug, and Cosmetic Act of 1938, is to be satisfied that a drug is *safe* before permitting it to be sold. The second, added by the Drug Amendments of 1962, requires evidence that a drug is *effective* in meeting the claims made by the manufacturer.

Most observers outside the drug industry believe that the FDA has not adequately carried out either responsibility, especially the latter. The typical view is that of W. Donald Gray, staff member of the House Intergovernmental Relations subcommittee, which has primary responsibility to oversee drug marketing and research: "The more knowledgeable I have become concerning the workings of the drug industry and the regulatory processes of the Food and Drug Administration, the more jaundiced I have become."[10]

10. W. Donald Gray, "The View from the Capitol," in Joseph D. Cooper (ed.), *The Economics of Drug Innovation* (American University, School of Business Administration, Center for the Study of Private Enterprise, 1970), pp. 20-21.

One problem confronting the FDA is a lack of cooperation from drug firms, which often fail to investigate drug safety and effectiveness in a scientific manner. According to the director of the Laboratory of Clinical Pharmacology at the Georgetown University School of Medicine, "The Achilles' heel of the system . . . is the nature and quality of the data describing the beneficial and adverse effects of the new drug in man. Repeatedly, the data submitted in support of New Drug Applications ignore a basic principle of applied medical research: the art of clinical investigation of the effects of drugs on man consists of the disciplined pursuit of systematic comparison under operational clinical conditions."[11]

Facing an industry that is not especially cooperative, the FDA has a difficult problem. Should it be relatively lax in authorizing the sale of drugs, thereby making sure that new drugs possessing important therapeutic advantages are distributed but risking the marketing of some unsafe or ineffective drugs? Or should it emphasize avoiding the latter at the expense of the former? While this is a difficult problem, most observers believe the FDA could be far tougher in dealing with the drug industry. The agency often takes a strangely neutral stance, as though the burden of proof should be on users or the medical profession to show that a drug is unsafe or ineffective. A 1971 case involving contaminated glassware containing liquids for intravenous feeding illustrates the attitude. The FDA did not place even a temporary embargo on use of the product until an investigation could be made, even though the investigation was to take only a few days.[12]

The reasons normally cited for the FDA's cautious behavior on drugs relate to the expertise and attitude of its staff. Martin believes the central problem to be that "virtually excluded from the decision-making process are the very individuals best-equipped to help make the decisions—experienced, productive scientists, both basic and clinical . . . whose independence and integrity are readily demonstrable."[13] An important reason for the FDA's lack of access to the persons best able to judge the scientific merits of a new drug is that the agency is a purely regulatory one. The FDA has little opportunity to engage in research and therefore has difficulty in attracting a good scientific staff. The top administrator of the agency has rarely had prior professional experience in food and drug problems. Even the minority of commissioners who have been pharmacists or physicians have generally not been well trained

11. Christopher M. Martin, "Reliability in Product Performance in an Innovative Environment," in Cooper, *The Economics of Drug Innovation*, p. 64.
12. See U.S. Department of Health, Education, and Welfare, Food and Drug Administration, "HEW News," 71-13, March 22, 1971.
13. "Reliability in Product Performance," p. 78.

in scientific research on product safety and effectiveness. Furthermore, the agency has not actively elicited support from the medical research and pharmacology community. In fact, one research director reports outright hostility within FDA toward researchers, especially before Goddard became chairman: "One had the feeling of working under conditions of an armed truce rather than one of mutual respect and cooperation."[14]

Finally, the FDA shares the problem of most regulatory agencies that most of the job opportunities available to their employees after they leave government service are in the regulated industry. This is bound to raise the suspicion that staff members are overly responsive, or at least subconsciously sympathetic, to the needs and claims of the industry simply because in the long run they will probably be working in the industry.

Other Consumer Protection Responsibilities

The FDA is also responsible for a wide variety of consumer protection activities. It has most recently been in the news with respect to toy safety and concentrations of mercury and other heavy metals in fish. As in the case of drug regulation, the FDA is often criticized as being too cautious and too protective of business. For example, the FDA waited about a year before taking any action on toy safety. Then, three shopping days before Christmas in 1970, it published a long list of toys regarded as unsafe—too late, of course, for the safety information to have much effect on Christmastime toy sales.[15] Furthermore, the FDA has the power to establish procedures whereby parents purchasing unsafe toys can receive a full refund of the purchase price; however, the FDA did not act under this authority, and so no provision was made for parents to return unsafe toys that they had purchased before the FDA list was published.

The case of the unsafe toys cannot be explained as easily as can the conservatism of the FDA with respect to food and drug regulation. While the latter may reflect the lack of scientific expertise in the agency, in most cases scientific expertise is hardly necessary for determining toy safety. Nor is the FDA staff likely to be interested in obtaining jobs in the toy business. Even the burst of energy that might be expected initially after the agency was assigned an entirely new responsibility—the so-called "Hawthorne effect"— does not appear to have materialized.

---

14. Irvine H. Page, "Discussion" (of Martin paper) in Cooper, *The Economics of Drug Innovation*, p. 86.
15. See "Uncle Sam Moves on Unsafe Toys (Slowly)," in *Consumer Reports*, Vol. 36 (March 1971), pp. 143-44.

Conclusions about the FDA

The FDA's procedures are not as legalistic as those of the independent commissions, and it is headed by a single administrator appointed by and serving at the pleasure of the President. Yet the agency does not appear to deserve high marks for its performance. While the FDA is housed in a large cabinet department, the constituency of that department—the medical and education professions—is not closely connected to the regulated industry; in fact, it is somewhat antipathetic to the regulated. Certainly the FDA case is one that needs explaining by proponents of executive-branch, single-administrator regulation.

Antitrust Enforcement

The Ash report proposes splitting the Federal Trade Commission into two components, one of which would inherit the antitrust responsibilities of the present agency. If this proposal is adopted, the federal government would have two offices within the President's administration devoted exclusively to antitrust activities—a new federal antitrust board and the present Antitrust division of the Department of Justice. Since both agencies would be part of the executive branch, the question arises as to why they should be separate.

At first glance, the agencies appear to have two differences, one of which is cited by the Ash Council. The FTC appears to be oriented toward economic issues—determining when a given business practice constitutes unfair competition—while the Antitrust division appears oriented toward legal issues, such as conspiracy among firms and absolute size of dominant firms. The Antitrust division is especially interested in activities that may be cause for criminal prosecution. The other apparent difference is that the FTC has certain formal court-like powers, whereas the Antitrust division receives publicity for launching court proceedings. The latter's public image is that of an advocate before a judicial body, while the former's is that of a decision-making, adjudicatory body.

In fact, these distinctions are not very real. Antitrust prosecution by the Justice Department is normally not a simple legal matter of size or conspiracy. The evidence supporting a claim that a "combination" is "in restraint of trade" or that an "attempt to monopolize" has taken place is often the "unfair trade practices" that the FTC is concerned about. The Antitrust division now relies heavily on economic expertise and has economists in important staff positions. In addition, the division, in effect, engages in administrative rule-

making. It often publishes guidelines as to what behavior constitutes grounds
for its taking legal action. Whether the behavior proscribed by the guidelines
would be upheld as illegal in a court is often uncertain, but nevertheless the
prudent businessman has a strong incentive not to risk antitrust prosecution
even if he could win. Furthermore, the division's cases often end in a consent
decree, an agreement between the Antitrust division and an individual or a
firm that the latter will cease a particular type of behavior of which the division disapproves, and in return that the former will not prosecute the latter
for past actions. Of course, the decision to grant a consent decree, rather than
engage in formal prosecution, is heavy with both policy and adjudicatory
implications. The Antitrust division behaves like an administrative body in
deciding when to seek a consent decree and what terms to include in it. By
the same token, the FTC becomes an advocate when its decisions are appealed
to the federal courts, as is common.

Both agencies have recognized the convergence of their activities and modes
of behavior. They recognize the potential for duplication of effort—or even
operation at cross-purposes—that is inherent in the present definition of responsibilities for both agencies. There is considerable informal cooperation between
the agencies, most notably an informal division of the industries to which each
agency will direct most of its attention. In practice, the two agencies have
come to represent a division of responsibility by industry, rather than by type
of offense or method of reform. (The main exception is enforcement of the
Robinson-Patman act, which has been left almost exclusively to the FTC.)
The initial divisions by industry were usually logical, based on the type of
anticompetitive problems within each industry. But as industry structures and
characteristics have changed, and especially as the competitive effect of mergers
has become an immensely important issue, the logic of the division of responsibility has been eroded.

The principal argument in favor of retaining the FTC's independence would
be that each of the agencies occasionally passes through a period of ineffectiveness, and that these periods do not necessarily coincide. Having two agencies
increases the likelihood that some antitrust enforcement will be proceeding
at an acceptable level most of the time. Bringing the FTC into the executive
branch, with the particularly close association with presidential politics implicit
in the proposal that one federal antitrust board member also be a member of
the Council of Economic Advisers, certainly would reduce the likelihood that
the two agencies would have greatly different antitrust prosecution policies
and degrees of activism.

Because of the similarity of responsibilities and functions, the past histories
of the two antitrust agencies also provide some basis for comparing alterna-

tive organizational structures. A summary view of professional opinion about the effectiveness of the two agencies is that, on balance, the Antitrust division has done considerably better in effectively promoting competition. Yet the division has also had a few periods when its performance is regarded as having been especially bad. For example, its performance during the last part of the Eisenhower administration receives generally good marks; but the marks are very low for the early Eisenhower period. When the Republicans took office in 1953, a number of extremely important and far-reaching antitrust cases were in process. Virtually all were settled through consent decrees that did not go as far as had been intended when the cases were opened. One example was the consent decree with AT&T, which preserved AT&T's ownership of Western Electric and the monopoly of AT&T business by Western Electric, in return for loosening up the equipment market for the independent telephone companies.[16] Since the consent decree, Western Electric has sold mainly to Bell operating companies and to the government, leaving the remaining market to other equipment manufacturers.

The 1953-56 performance of the Antitrust division illustrates the problem of substantially increasing presidential control over regulatory agencies. Policy can be quite discontinuous in philosophy and in the tenacity with which it is applied, and a short period of lapse can have important consequences that are difficult, if not impossible, to overcome.

The FTC's reputation for weaker enforcement could be attributed to the directions it has been given, rather than to its organizational form. Early court cases testing FTC actions placed extremely narrow interpretations on the FTC's mandate,[17] and the Robinson-Patman Act was "at least potentially inconsistent with the general body of antitrust laws."[18]

Two conclusions can be drawn from the comparative analysis of the two antitrust agencies. First, incorporation within the executive and a single administrator do not guarantee a strong, effective agency, as the periods of moribund behavior by the Antitrust division show. Second, the distinctions in the responsibilities, powers, and orientations of the two agencies, whatever initial logic they had, are becoming so blurred as to lose meaning.

The Ash Council proposal would seem to sacrifice the principal advantage of having two agencies (a greater chance that somewhere in government some

16. The consent decree was entered Jan. 24, 1956, in the United States District Court of New Jersey.

17. See *FTC* v. *Gratz,* 253 U.S. 421 (1920), which Carl Kaysen and Donald F. Turner, in *Antitrust Policy* (Harvard University Press, 1959), argue "repressed for nearly two decades whatever creative urges the Federal Trade Commission might otherwise have had" (p. 237).

18. *Ibid.,* p. 239.

agency will be promoting competition) without eliminating the principal dis-advantage (duplication of responsibility and effort).

The Regulation of Banking*

Bank regulation in the United States is carried on by many agencies with many different organizational forms and thereby offers a rich opportunity for investigating the Ash report's premise that performance is closely connected with structure. Federal regulation of banking is intimately connected with a complex pattern of banking regulation by the states.

At the heart of bank regulation is the concept of the "dual banking sys-tem"—federal and state regulation of banks. Although the dual system has too often been used as a shibboleth to protect vested interests, the concept is not lacking in cogent rationale. The division of powers between the federal govern-ment and the states in this field has provided a set of checks and balances that has served to limit the concentration of economic power in the banking indus-try, though it has not necessarily resulted in the economically most efficient solutions.

The Federal Agencies

The federal bank-regulatory structure includes at least three and perhaps four types of regulatory agencies: (1) The Comptroller of the Currency is not usually recognized as an independent federal regulator, his office having been established before the concept was well defined; but to a large extent his office has the powers of an independent regulatory agency. (2) The Board of Gover-nors of the Federal Reserve System—in its regulatory role, as distinguished from its monetary policy role—has taken on more and more the characteristics of an independent regulatory agency. (3) The Federal Deposit Insurance Cor-poration (FDIC) is essentially an administrative agency headed by a three-man board, of which one member is the Comptroller of the Currency. The role of the chairman of the FDIC has become stronger over the years, and the FDIC is very close to being an agency with a single administrator. (4) Since 1966 the Department of Justice has played a rather large role in the regulation of the banking industry through its power to obtain an automatic stay of pro-posed mergers and holding-company acquisitions.

Any comparison of these agencies on the basis of the relationship between structure and performance is subject to considerable qualification. The follow-ing observations are offered without concern for the qualifications, although

*This section was contributed by Charles F. Haywood.

this has inherent risks. The Comptroller of the Currency is somewhat more an advocate of banking interests than are the other agencies named above. The Comptroller has not been lax in surveillance and enforcement, but he has sought to relax restrictions limiting the expansion of banks. He is not averse to doing battle with other agencies, particularly the Department of Justice, on behalf of individual banks as well as of the industry at large. There is more informality in the Comptroller's dealings with the banks he regulates, and in most instances he effects decisions and actions more quickly than do the other agencies. Over the past decade or so the Comptroller has been the major force for change in the structure of the banking industry and for expanding the powers of commercial banks. The experience suggests that a single official having something close to the powers and status of an independent regulatory agency can be more responsive to needs for change in an industry than can an independent regulatory agency headed by a board, or an administrative agency headed by a board or a single official.

State Regulation

Several years ago a study of the state bank-regulatory authorities was made to determine the extent to which such authorities have the powers and status of an independent regulatory agency.[19] Nine characteristics of an independent regulatory agency were used as criteria. Extensive interviews were held with state bank supervisors, and state banking statutes and administrative procedure codes were reviewed. It was found that the state banking departments could be classified into four categories: (a) one department (Virginia) with the powers and status of an independent regulatory agency; (b) nine departments with some of the powers of an independent regulatory agency; (c) twenty-nine departments which are ministerial but enjoy some degree of independence vis-a-vis the governor's office; and (d) eleven ministerial departments that appear to have significantly limited independence. In a number of instances the state fell into category (c) largely because of the strength of the current governor or of the individual who served as state bank supervisor.

The state banking department in Virginia had not made full use of its powers as an independent regulatory agency, and in practice it functioned the same as did the nine departments in category (b). These ten departments were all among the more effective state banking authorities in the nation. Of the eleven departments in category (d), nine were judged among the weakest in the nation. In the twenty-nine states in category (c), the effectiveness of the authority was very much a function of the attitude of current and past gover-

19. Carter H. Golembe and Charles F. Haywood, "A Study of the Responsibilities and Powers Delegated to State Banking Authorities" (unpublished manuscript, 1968).

nors, the personal capabilities of current and past supervisors and chief deputies, and the willingness of the banking industry in the state to support effective regulation, both morally and financially.

On the basis of this study, the following generalizations can be made: (1) Effective regulation appears to be served when the regulatory authority is an independent unit and is effectively insulated from partisan political pressures. (2) Where the regulatory authority does not clearly have independent status, the effectiveness of regulation depends very much on personal attitudes and capabilities. (3) Where some degree of independence is assured, the authority appears better able to attract and retain capable staff as well as supervisors and chief deputies. (4) While performance in the less independent agencies is occasionally as effective as in those that are more independent, in general the less independent agencies tend to have less capable personnel and to be less effective in the performance of regulatory responsibilities.

The Need for Competition

The regulation of commercial banking has been directed mainly to preventing bank failures—that is, to protecting the public in maintaining a sound banking structure rather than a "tariff schedule" of services and prices. In personal interviews with state bank supervisors, several questions were asked to elicit information about the extent to which state banking departments were concerned about the quality and price of banking services. In states that permit statewide branch banking, supervisors felt that competition was adequate to assure that the public convenience and need would be served. In states that prohibit branch banking or permit it on a limited geographical basis, some supervisors were concerned about the need for supervision to be directed toward the quality and price of banking services. This finding tends to support the view that the key reform in the regulation of commercial banks today would be the further relaxation of restrictions limiting competition. Making regulation more effective, either in dealing with anticompetitive practices or in setting standards of performance, appears much less important.

The Tariff Commission*

The Ash Council did not have the Tariff Commission in mind when writing its report. Nevertheless, some of the Council's general observations do fit the commission, while others do not.

* This section was contributed by Lawrence B. Krause.

The Tariff Commission was established by legislation in 1916. It is a relic of an era when tariff treaties did not exist. At that time U.S. tariffs were set by the Congress in response to an alleged need for protection. In fact, tariffs were a partisan issue. During Republican administrations, tariffs were generally increased; during Democratic administrations, they were usually reduced. There was spreading awareness that the Congress had very little solid information on which to base its tariff-making and a belief developed that tariff-making could be put on a scientific basis. The so-called scientific tariff gave every industry enough protection to permit it to compete with imports; that is, the amount of a tariff equalled the difference between foreign and domestic costs of production. The fact that this did not make economic sense (it would eliminate all the benefits of trade) did not seem to bother those who suggested that this method of setting tariffs was superior to the earlier political log-rolling method.

The Tariff Commission was given three tasks. The first was to advise the Congress on technical matters, costs of production, and the like. The second was to make recommendations to the Congress when requested. The third was to provide information to the President that was needed to administer special aspects of the tariff laws. To perform these tasks, a commission of six members was established, the members having overlapping terms. The commissioners were to be appointed by the President and confirmed by the Senate. To guarantee the nonpartisan nature of the tariff investigations, the Congress stipulated that not more than three members of the commission could come from the same political party. Three Democrats and three Republicans have made up the commission since its inception.

In current circumstances the Congress does not try to legislate tariff rate changes, except in very unusual circumstances, since most U.S. tariffs are now included in presidential agreements with other countries. The remaining task left to the Tariff Commission is to advise the President in certain escape-clause cases and dumping cases that the President has to administer under the existing tariff laws. This in essence means that the Tariff Commission is no longer primarily an investigative body but one that has to make substantive determinations of injury in certain circumstances.

The point made by the Ash Council that regulatory commissions have not been sufficiently responsive to economic, technological, structural, and social change is certainly true of the Tariff Commission. The Trade Expansion Act of 1962 provided for adjustment assistance for workers who were displaced by imports. Because of its excessively legalistic approach, the Tariff Commission has been reluctant to grant findings of need for adjustment, despite the fact that this is now recognized as an important welfare requirement when tariffs are being reduced. Excessive legalism results from being responsive to the Congress and not to the President directly. Unlike other commissions, however, the Tariff Commission is accountable because of its advisory nature; it does not make binding determinations, and its findings are public knowledge. Still the Tariff Commission is not sufficiently coordinated with national policy goals, as the lack of adjustment assistance findings clearly points out.

From an organizational point of view, having six commissioners is ridiculous. Because substantive findings are now required from the commission, having an equal number of commissioners from each political party frequently leads to three-to-three splits. A reduction of the Tariff Commission to three members, with one being designated chairman and having operating responsibilities, would be an improvement over the present six-member commission. Further, the requirement of nonpartisanship no longer has meaning, since attitudes toward tariff policies are no longer along party lines; having three Democrats and three Republicans does not guarantee ideological balance, as once was the case.

Indeed what is required are honest men, and this need can best be met by giving responsibility to a smaller number. The commission has had difficulty in attracting and retaining highly qualified commissioners. At times eminent people have accepted appointments only to leave after a short time. With such limited responsibilities, it is unlikely that highly qualified persons would accept positions as commissioners. It may well be that the whole commission idea should be abolished, with the President setting up an investigative office within the executive offices to assist him in meeting his requirements under the tariff laws.

Fuel Prices and the Regulatory Agencies*

In discussing power regulation, the Ash Council—as elsewhere in its report—deals with organizational and political problems, not with economic issues. Nevertheless, the economic issues influence one's appraisal of the report. If the recommended changes in organization would not improve economic performance in cases where it is now inadequate, perhaps even more sweeping and imaginative changes are needed.

The following analysis deals with the regulation of fuels and energy: oil, natural gas, coal, and electric power generated from these fuels and from

* This section was contributed by James W. McKie.

atomic energy. These sources of energy are sold in an interrelated, though differentiated, set of markets. Public policy toward them inevitably influences their markets and their relations to each other; policies ought to be coordinated, if not unified, to take account of these relationships.

Oil

The main factors affecting prices and markets of crude oil and derived products are oil import controls and state-administered production controls on U.S. output. (Federal tax policies—the depletion allowance and the privilege of expensing intangible drilling costs—also have some influence, though less than they formerly had.)

Oil import controls. Quotas on oil imports sustain a difference of about $1.25 to $1.50 a barrel in normal times between the price of U.S. domestic crude and the delivered cost of imported oil. This price differential does not appear in heavy residual fuel oil, which is exempt from the quota on the East Coast, where most of it is used. Residual oil sells at world prices. It is the petroleum product that is most closely substitutable for coal and is an important fuel in electric power generation and other industrial uses. Domestic refiners produce very little residual fuel oil, and would produce little more even if it were subject to quota restrictions.

The Oil Import Administration (OIA), an administrative unit located in the Department of the Interior, has played an important, though diminishing, role in setting oil-importation policy. The agency is headed by an administrator, assisted by a deputy administrator and three assistant administrators, and has no other professional staff. It is not strictly a regulatory commission, but it formerly had some points of resemblance to the kind of regulatory organization envisioned by the Ash report. (It was stripped of some of its functions in February 1970.)

The OIA was never a policy-determining body on large issues. The President has direct authority to impose restrictions on imports for reasons of national security, and the overall policy has emerged from a classic convergence of political pressures involving the White House, the Congress, industry groups (including the hybrid industry-government National Petroleum Council), and other executive offices, such as the Office of Oil and Gas in the Department of the Interior. All changes in the regulations, before 1970, were issued by the secretary of the interior. Nevertheless, the OIA certainly participated in setting major policy guidelines; and on smaller matters and administrative rules, it was the dominant agency. For example, maintaining the "sliding scale" rules favoring small refiners and setting rules to govern the administration of allocations to petrochemical producers were largely within its competence, though outside pressures also played a role. The exemption of residual oil and the special status given to imports from Canada, being larger questions, probably were influenced more by constituencies outside the OIA.

The Presidential Proclamation of 1959 limiting imports also set up an Oil Import Appeals Board, located in the Department of the Interior and consisting of representatives of the Departments of the Interior, Defense, and Commerce.[20] It had the power to modify or grant new allocations (in addition to the historic ones), on grounds of hardship or error, from a "set-aside" quantity of import rights deducted from the total import quota of crude oil and petroleum products.

In February 1970, jurisdiction over oil import policy (more exactly, the power to make recommendations to the President) was transferred to the Oil Policy Committee, headed by the director of the Office of Emergency Preparedness. (One unstated aim of this change was to reduce the influence of the Department of the Interior over oil policy.) Since then the OIA has continued to administer the program and to participate in the meetings of the Oil Policy Committee, but policy and rules are determined by the whole committee. Some recent actions taken by the committee would probably not have been initiated or approved by the OIA.

During the time when the OIA had more discretion than it has now, its administration of the overall policy was almost wholly in the interests of the petroleum industry, reflecting the commitment of the Department of the Interior and the executive branch itself. One must recognize the ostensible aim of the program—the protection of national security. Most observers agree that unlimited dependence on foreign oil is not in the national interest. But at the inception of the Mandatory Oil Import Program in 1959 the security requirement was translated into a quota limitation of about 12.5 percent of domestic production east of the Rockies (modified for the West Coast) and was never changed substantially thereafter. In establishing these guidelines, the agency never made any attempt to define adequately the security parameters of the oil import policy and fought most attempts to liberalize it. The OIA came to be regarded as industry-oriented almost to the same degree as the Office of Oil and Gas. Its major concern with conflict of interests was in mediating among factions within the petroleum industry. But its major inadequacies of economic performance should really be ascribed to the executive office, which determined the main elements of policy in the first place and which could have overridden the OIA at any time. Perhaps this illustrates the

20. Presidential Proclamation 3279, March 10, 1959, sec. 4.

shortcomings of a regulatory agency that is under the direct control of the executive; it is difficult to see how the performance of the OIA was any better than if it had been an independent regulatory agency.

Prorationing. "Market demand" prorationing by the states has the effect of stabilizing crude oil prices, at least relatively. It also helps to sustain price increases, though price competition often erodes the effect of production stabilization. State control agencies usually are passive stabilizers; they seldom have tried to push prices up by cutting back output on their own initiative.

The net effect of both of these policies is to make the prices of oil and oil products (other than heavy fuel oil) considerably higher in the United States than they would be otherwise, though the effect is diminished somewhat by favorable tax treatment. The consumption of light heating oil, a fuel with important substitutes, is discouraged. The effect of higher oil prices on the supply of natural gas is not easy to measure, but since the two fuels are to some degree joint products, the supply of gas is doubtless enhanced. Higher oil prices mean lower gas prices, other things being equal. And the difference in policy between heavy fuel oil and other petroleum products may lead to some substitution of the former for competitive fuels—and also substitution of electric power generated from residual oil.

Natural Gas

Consumer gas prices are regulated by state and local public utility commissions. The exception is gas that is supplied directly from interstate pipelines to major industrial users, which is exempt from regulation. The Federal Power Commission controls the prices of natural gas sold to utilities by interstate pipelines and also imposes ceilings on the field prices of gas sold to interstate pipelines by independent producers.

Critics have raised some questions about FPC regulation of pipeline rates. The zone differentials may not adequately measure distance cost differentials, and the so-called "Atlantic Seaboard formula" used to allocate costs to mainline industrial users (unregulated) may discriminate against those users. But these questions are trivial compared to the main one—the ceilings on field prices of natural gas. The FPC has fixed such ceilings for producing areas on the basis of the aggregate costs of the principal producers in each area, without reference to the effect of such prices on supply or demand. The producing industry has a substantially competitive structure and probably operates under classic conditions of increasing costs. Under the conditions that have recently prevailed—increasing cost, disappearing uncommitted reserves, and booming demand—the effect of the FPC policy has been to discourage the development of new supply (price is probably below long-run marginal cost in most areas) and to stimulate unduly the growth of certain kinds of demand, notably industrial and utility demand for boiler fuel. The latter effect is most visible in areas, such as the Middle West, that were beneficiaries of the earlier very low price ceilings set in the 1950s, but it is present elsewhere. A secondary effect of FPC price regulation has been to divert gas supplies to the unregulated intrastate market and perhaps to distort industrial location patterns.

For some years the consequences of price ceilings that are below the long-run equilibrium were staved off by the absorption of uncommitted earlier discoveries and a decline in the ratio of reserves to production. The crisis arrived in 1970, after several years of failure by the industry to replace annual production, and the decline in reserve ratios reached levels so low as to endanger deliverability. The FPC has shown a renewed interest in price incentives. If these are not successful in time, or if they are not applied in sufficient degree, then the control authority may have to resort to end-use rationing. The commission has already hinted that such controls may be necessary in any event.

The net social cost of misallocating resources by making gas unduly cheap and the subsidy to consumers are impossible to calculate, though they are undoubtedly smaller than the social costs and transfers to the industry resulting from the excess of domestic prices of oil over world prices.[21] On the production end, the artificially depressed price of natural gas acts as a drag on oil development to the extent that they are joint products; but this drag does not nearly offset the artificial stimulus stemming from the domestic oil price differential.

Electric Power

Apart from hydroelectric power, the significance of which is limited and diminishing, electric power costs at present largely reflect the relative costs of the fuels discussed below. The big unknown for the future is nuclear power. The promotional policies and controls of the Atomic Energy Commission (AEC) have played the dominant role in nuclear power development, which has not measured up to the expectations of fifteen years ago; but now environmental considerations are coming insistently to the fore, and the environmental control agencies will in the future have an important voice in determining the

21. Of course the latter cost is offset to some extent by a benefit: national security against an interruption of foreign supply. But leaving this out of account, the costs and transfers associated with the oil program are well over $4 billion a year at present. If gas is priced 20 percent below its equilibrium value—a not unreasonable assumption at present—the gross transfers and costs probably do not exceed $1 billion.

relative costs of all power generation methods and hence the growth of nuclear energy. Finally, the AEC and the State Department are interested in controlling the international diffusion of technology under the Nuclear Nonproliferation Treaty, signed by the United States in 1969, and other arrangements. These could have an effect on U.S. development of controlled fusion, breeder reactors, and so on, and ultimately on the price of electricity.

Coal

Although it is not a regulated industry, coal mining is influenced by a multitude of public policies, some of which have significant effects on coal prices. Government-supported cartelization of the industry has repeatedly been sought, beginning with the Guffey Coal Act of 1935. Most recently the Federal Coal Mine Health and Safety Act of 1969—a long-overdue action to force the industry to bear a cost it had transferred to its workers—has altered the structure of the industry considerably and raised coal prices substantially. Government has also moved to control exports (during the threatened shortage in the winter of 1970-71); and in the future, environmental policies will exert increasing upward pressure on the cost of coal. These policies have already had a powerful indirect effect on the costs of electric power, and this is undoubtedly just the beginning.[22]

Policy Coordination

The melange of policies toward energy, which are briefly summarized here, can hardly be called rational or consistent. Some policies increase energy prices, others decrease them; some result in misallocation of resources and generation of social costs, while others are designed to correct misallocation; most policies on individual fuels take little or no account of their effects on other sectors of the energy economy.

"Regulation" of energy is diffuse. Although most of the agencies making energy policies were not within the purview of the Ash Council, the Council was aware of the general coordination problem. On the question of "coordinated response," the Ash report says:

Some decisions and responsibilities of the FPC require a recognition of the interrelated activities and interests of other governmental agencies. For example, the FPC's jurisdiction over interstate aspects of electrical energy generally does not extend to fuel sources (except for gas) necessary for generating elec-

22. During the past four years, TVA electric rates have risen 50 percent. Cost factors associated with the 1969 mine safety act, growing export demand, and TVA's loss of monopsony power account for most of the rate increase.

tricity. Availability and the price of oil, coal, and nuclear fuels—now comprising 73 percent of fuel needs for the generation of electricity—are affected by decisions of other Federal agencies, thus making interagency coordination essential. In the future, this need will become more acute, since it is estimated that, by 1980, 83 percent of the requirements may be served by these fuels.

As Commissioner John A. Carver, Jr. has noted: "Today the critical aspects of utility operations are at least as likely to be the subject of proceedings before the SEC, AEC, Interior, Justice, HEW, or some component thereof, as before the FPC." Yet interagency coordination, difficult under the best of circumstances, becomes almost impossible when handled through representatives of a commission which must reach agreement before action can be taken. A single administrator, relieved of the obligation to negotiate compromises, would find it easier to commit the agency to a decided course and delegate authority to subordinates participating in coordination efforts.[23]

If the Ash Council had considered the entire organization of "energy policy" in making specific recommendations, it would have been in a better position to promote consistency in policy than it was after considering only proposals for reorganizing the FPC. Possibly a single administrator for the FPC could coordinate more expeditiously, but the proposal does nothing to resolve the different interests and constituencies that produce different policies, nor to provide any means of reconciling the results. Energy and fuel prices would continue to be under the influence of conflicting policies, which are only partly embodied in regulation by an independent agency. One may legitimately doubt whether the Ash proposal is likely to bring the whole energy sector much closer to the goal of economic efficiency.

The Federal Power Commission*

As applied to the Federal Power Commission, the Ash report's recommendations on organizational structure could achieve the goals for which they are designed. Yet the chances that organizational changes will bring important substantive changes in the performance of regulated power and gas companies do not seem great.

The importance of protecting the public from the monopoly power or pricing policies of gas pipeline companies and electric companies is diminishing in comparison with the importance of achieving coordinated, long-range governmental planning to secure future energy supplies. The need for more energy is

---

*This section was contributed by Paul W. MacAvoy and Stephen Breyer.

23. The President's Advisory Council on Executive Organization, *A New Regulatory Framework: Report on Selected Independent Regulatory Agencies* (1971), p. 111.

well known—there are persistent and significant demands in excess of peak capacity in electricity and gas in the large population centers—as is the effect of energy generation in damaging and polluting the environment. This potential conflict between competing public desires requires careful analysis, balance of interests, and public political decision. Moreover, to achieve any given level of energy requirements with maximum economic efficiency and minimum environmental harm calls for coordinated planning, and because of the external nature of the environmental costs, this should involve the public.

The present FPC has not anticipated or helped to resolve these problems. Indeed, the National Power Survey, completed in 1964, helped to allay fears that the problems were serious.[24] The FPC played an important role in creating the national gas shortage;[25] in fact, the commission has only recently begun to face the long-run effects that its gas field price ceilings have on supply. In the future, with a reconstructed FPC, commission pricing decisions might be viewed not independently, but as part of longer-range planning for energy needs. The Ash report speaks of the need for more policy planning; it is surely as pressing a need in the FPC as in any regulatory commission.

Although divisiveness has not been a serious problem in the FPC, planning decisions, which involve tradeoffs between energy supply and environmental quality, probably should be political decisions made by an elected official rather than semijudicial decisions approving engineering reports by commission staff. Divisiveness aside, there has been a tendency for decisions to favor regulated electricity and gas transporters relative to the retailers or consumers.[26]

The proposal to replace the commission with one man, responsible to the President, seems a step in the right direction. Locating policy decisions in the executive branch should increase political accountability, and, insofar as these decisions are seen as important to voters' groups, it should diminish industry influence. Moreover, power planning will require legislation and greater coordination among various government departments, for which strong executive branch support may prove necessary.

Freeing the agency chief to some extent from his adjudicatory responsibility also seems promising, if only to a limited degree. At present, the commission must review many cases. Applications for certificates to build

24. *National Power Survey,* A Report by the Federal Power Commission, 1964 (Government Printing Office, 1964).

25. Paul W. MacAvoy, "The Regulation-Induced Shortage of Natural Gas," *Journal of Law and Economics* (Spring 1971).

26. Paul W. MacAvoy, "The Formal Work-Product of the Federal Power Commissioners," *Bell Journal of Economics and Management Science,* Vol. 2 (Spring 1971), pp. 379-95.

additional service facilities, for example, may run to more than 300 a year, and each receives a formal case review before the commissioners—even though these are of trivial importance; and, while review has often been made routine, it is still time-consuming. The commissioners have persisted in publishing a thousand pages of these cases each year, even though no more than 10 percent establish a policy or even have an effect on the regulated firms.[27] Even the cases critical to the specific firm involved—such as those on the allowed rate of return on capital—contain little of substance for other firms because the commissioners do not follow consistent and observable decision rules. Yet 100-page examiner's decisions and thousands of pages of testimony are given a full case review and decision every time. Since nothing would be lost, the FPC might well pay more attention to longer-range policy and planning.

The Impact of the Ash Proposals

While the Ash report proposals appear to have some potential benefits, the importance of the recommended changes does not appear very great, for several reasons:

1. Placing an agency under the direct control of the President will not necessarily produce "better" policy. No theory of political accountability says that quadrennial presidential elections guarantee more enlightened policy in any specific agency, and no empirical laws predict that commissions make better policies when switched from "independent" to "executive" status. One need only compare the statements on the "energy crisis" by the assistant secretary of the interior for mineral resources[28] with those by the chairman of the Federal Power Commission[29] to see that agency "location" does not necessarily affect agency policy (or its "quality"). Accountability to the President is one factor, but the power of the Congress over the agency's expenditures (as in Interior) and the power of the industry in the executive branch are others.

2. The formulation of energy policy may inevitably be an ad hoc or sequential process. The making of policy involving energy generation and environmental quality probably requires, in addition to generalized policy statements, close attention to the siting of individual power plants. That is, it may not prove possible to develop any but the most general rules for choosing proportions of fuel supplies without detailed analyses of the political elements in specific plant sites. If so, policy will be made in part through individual case

27. *Ibid.*

28. Hollis M. Dole, "America's Energy Needs and Resources" (address delivered at Stanford University, Jan. 12, 1971).

29. John N. Nassikas, testimony before the Subcommittee on Minerals, Materials and Fuels of the Senate Committee on the Interior and Insular Affairs, Nov. 13, 1969.

decisions. The proposed federal power agency would inevitably, and rightly, be drawn into these decisions, but the process of policy making could not be carried out within the Ash Council structure. Any thirty-day review require-ment, as applied to such cases, would prove unworkable; similarly, the pro-posed hearing examiner-administrative court channel for adjudication and review would probably not prove feasible for important pipeline certification proceedings or gas area rate proceedings where the results depended upon policies of exploitation of nuclear and petroleum fuels. The more specialized the attention required in making important power policies—and the more interrelated the fuel markets become as policy making becomes more con-sistent—the less significant will be the report's proposals for separating adjudi-cation from general policy formulation.

The thirty-day time limit on agency review is one of many detailed com-ponents of the plan for reorganization that seems arbitrary. No evidence is presented to show that this time period has been or would be better than other time periods. It might be better to have no time limit at all, but rather to have a presidential appointee who seeks to make policy by building a con-sistent case record.

3. That many different jurisdictions divide responsibility for the public supervision of power is a far more important obstacle to coordinated planning than any factor that the Ash report discusses. To take but one recent example, before Consolidated Edison could build a twenty-five mile extension of a 345 kilovolt transmission line, it had to obtain approval from eight municipalities, the Hudson River Valley Commission, the Federal Aviation Administration, the Army Corps of Engineers, the New York State Highway Department, the East Hudson Parkway Authority, and the Palisades Interstate Park Commis-sion. Such a process not only wastes time, but also gives a power company every incentive to plan expansion with the aim in mind simply of minimizing the delays and costs of the administrative proceedings. Division of responsi-bility between state and federal agencies in setting electricity prices has pro-duced similar, but more manageable problems, although it has also resulted in systems of less than optimal scale and in little price regulation.[30] The Ash proposals provide no relief from these problems.

4. The report's proposals are not likely to improve the FPC's "profit regu-lation" performance. During some periods in the 1960s, when marginal costs were above average costs, the FPC probably allowed pipeline companies to

30. MacAvoy, "The Formal Work-Product of the Federal Power Commissioners," and William R. Hughes, "Scale Frontiers in Electric Power," in William M. Capron (ed.), *Technological Change in Regulated Industries* (Brookings Institution, 1971).

earn average rates of return that were well above the marginal costs of capital.[31] Presumably the staff involved would be unchanged if the Ash proposals were implemented, and it is difficult to believe that an Administrative Court would delve deeply into such a technical matter as capital costs. Thus the only hope is for the administrator of the proposed federal power agency to promulgate rules requiring quantitative evidence on financial costs and use of the evidence to reduce excess profits. The hopes are slim, on grounds of capacity to handle the evidence alone.

Conclusion

The Ash report offers little comment on the economic substance of regulation. Some attention is paid to agency delay, and the (implied) social costs of delays, but that is all. Insofar as changes in economic policy would entail recommendations for new legislation, it may make good sense to focus on structural changes instead, since the latter may have a better chance of congressional approval. But any such hope is limited by the very indirect relation between the proposed federal power agency operations and the new economic policy required.

The very process of change itself may improve performance, for it may provoke a reexamination of old policies and force the development of new ones. In fact, most commission mandates—including those of the FPC—are broadly stated and allow the commissions considerable flexibility in formulating and revising general policy. Perhaps just threatening the FPC with the Ash Council proposals would cause it to respond by finally solving the problems it faces in gas supplies and electricity capacity.

Regulation in the Department of Agriculture*

It is difficult to generalize about the many regulatory activities of the Department of Agriculture, either as reflected in the Ash Council recommendations or as measured by the success of regulation in meeting certain economic and social criteria.

The Department of Agriculture is literally swamped with regulatory functions, administering about fifty separate pieces of regulatory legislation. Many of these are not even conceived of as antitrust or regulatory functions by

*This section was contributed by James Bonnen.
31. MacAvoy, "The Formal Work-Product of the Federal Power Commissioners," pp. 384-88.

those who execute them. Attention will be focused here on three of the more important regulatory activities.

The Price Support System

Two agencies of the Department of Agriculture are responsible essentially for regulating prices of certain politically important agricultural commodities—the Commodity Credit Corporation (CCC) and the Agricultural Stabilization and Conservation Service (ASCS). The CCC is a guaranteed-loan and stockpile operation that makes nonrecourse loans to cooperating farmers. The CCC, using the crop as collateral, loans to farmers the value of their crop at the target price and contracts to purchase the crop in the event that market prices fall below the target. If that happens, the CCC removes from the market those stocks that are "excess" at the target price level. The target price is a guaranteed minimum price to all who cooperate in the program by limiting their planting to an acreage allotment set by the Department of Agriculture. CCC does not set the price targets, but merely acts to insure that price targets determined elsewhere are reached.

Formerly the specific price targets were often set by the agricultural committees of the Congress. The farm commodity interests have always worked to reduce their market uncertainties by limiting the discretion of the secretary of agriculture and the administrator of ASCS in setting price targets and acreage allotments.

Increasingly, as there has been a dilution in the power of farmers within the farm bloc in the Congress, congressional committees have found it more difficult to reach such decisions. In the past, producers exercised nearly complete power through the committees, but in recent years other food and fiber industry groups have caused that power to be fragmented. Consequently the decision-making power has been pushed toward the Department of Agriculture. Under legislation passed in 1965, Agriculture has had substantial discretionary power in setting prices, though the Agricultural Act of 1970 has dissipated much of that discretion.

Nevertheless, policy and enforcement action are not necessarily focused in the same offices. The secretary of agriculture has the main voice in setting targets; his staff work is done at several points in the department, with ASCS often the primary source. The executive office and the White House usually are involved in the major price support policy decisions; their influence is sometimes a major constraint on the department and on the Congress. The administrator of ASCS translates the targets into actions on marketing quotas and acreage controls; the CCC picks up the general targets from the secretary and the specific actions of the ASCS to set its own pattern of purchases and sales of commodities. This means that the agencies enforcing the regulatory rules really do not have primary control over policy and rate-making decisions. The latter are made through a political process that involves the Congress, the White House, and the cabinet-level executive branch officials. This is where one can most legitimately quarrel with the process. While many believe that price-support policies are misdirected, rarely are the CCC and ASCS criticized for ineffectiveness in executing these policies.

The Commodity Exchange Authority

The Commodity Exchange Authority makes and administers the rules governing futures markets in food products. Although it is an agency under the secretary of agriculture, it operates with considerable independence, in part because it has been consistently well directed and has seldom aroused controversy. It is one of the most effective regulatory agencies in the federal government.

The authority's success reflects the nature of its functions, which include authorizing futures markets in certain farm commodities, licensing brokers, prescribing trading rules, enforcing rules on speculative trading,[32] and ensuring that the exchanges enforce their own rules. These functions are supported by a highly effective information system that keeps the authority in daily touch with developments in the exchanges and brokerage firms. Because the authority is prepared to anticipate problems—for instance, a deteriorating financial situation in a firm—most of its business is preventive and is transacted informally. Even its formal actions are administrative: few problems end up in the courts.

The authority is seldom called upon to transfer wealth from one party to another. In other words, it referees very few zero-sum games. Since nearly all of the players gain from maintaining the integrity of the futures markets, the Commodity Exchange Authority is usually viewed as wearing the "white hat," while the persons whose behavior it constrains are seen as "black hats"—even by those being regulated.

The authority does not regulate prices or exert substantive control of entry. It simply makes and enforces the rules of a game in which political power is balanced and the constituency is broad. An important consequence of the relative freedom from conflict enjoyed by the authority is that it has had only

---

32. Rules on speculative trading are established by the Commodity Exchange Commission, composed of the secretary of agriculture, the secretary of commerce, and the attorney general. In practice, the commission rarely meets and normally only reviews decisions by the administrator of the Commodity Exchange Authority.

four administrators in the fifty years since it was founded in 1922. The current administrator has been in office for eleven years. This stability of tenure has enabled the agency to attract outstanding leadership.

The Packers and Stockyards Administration

The Packers and Stockyards Administration (PSA) has antitrust and trade practice responsibilities with respect to meat packers and poultry firms that are comparable to those of the FTC with respect to industry generally. The PSA's authority also extends to public utility regulation of stockyards and to regulating the trade practices of dealers and other persons trading in livestock throughout the United States. The agency is quite often in hot water politically.

The political atmosphere in which the PSA operates has no doubt contributed to a series of short-term administrators. Since passage of the Packers and Stockyards Act in 1921, the political winds have carried it from the status of a separate agency reporting directly to the secretary of agriculture down to a branch of a division of an agency—and finally in 1967 back to its present position as a separate agency.

Economic conflicts in the PSA's regulatory field are direct and frequent. The interests of the farmer and the packer (or poultry firm) are diametrically opposed, for they compete for the income from livestock (or poultry) production. These conflicts take place in a $20 billion a year industry that accounts for about one-third of farm income and consumer expenditures for farm foods.

Originally the PSA role was to protect farmers against monopolistic and sharp practices in meat packing and livestock marketing. The agency was formed because it was believed that the packing industry was exploiting farmers. Today it tries to protect all parties and has acquired a complex legislative mandate. The structure of the packing and livestock industries has changed drastically, but PSA has been able to adjust only slowly to the change. It has also reacted very slowly to the current tide of consumer complaints. Some criticize the agency for setting inappropriate goals; but the heart of the matter is a failure, indeed, often a political inability, even to consider the impact of agency actions beyond the limited scope of the market they regulate.

With its great range of responsibilities, not only does PSA often find itself refereeing substantial economic conflicts, but it also faces a political situation in which power is unequally distributed. This makes the agency vulnerable to industry retaliation. Thirty years ago farmers had a voice in all agricultural policy matters that food and fiber marketing firms could not hope to offset. Today the balance of political power in marketing food and fiber lies with the trade organizations of the meat packers, the poultry processors, and the marketing cooperatives. The only hope for political balance in the future lies in developing the countervailing power of consumer interest.

The most recent PSA administrator was one of the more aggressive the agency has had in recent years. He had substantial support from Secretary Orville L. Freeman, who strongly supported the regulatory activities of the Department of Agriculture. In addition, the last administrator had had civil service status in his previous position, and the Civil Service Commission refused to permit his civil service security to be removed when he was made PSA administrator. Consequently he was guaranteed an equivalent job within the government even if he was removed as agency administrator. The present incumbent has only the usual status of a political appointee, and even though he is very able, it is doubtful that he could ever have as much freedom as his predecessor enjoyed. In any case, if he is as aggressive, his tenure could be even shorter.

Both the Commodity Exchange Authority and PSA are unlike independent regulatory agencies, since their most important responsibilities are shared with other offices. Neither agency has its own legal counsel. The Office of the General Counsel to the secretary of agriculture performs all legal counsel functions. Hearing examiners are also located in the secretary's office rather than in the agencies, as is the judicial officer, who hears appeals and speaks for the secretary in imposing any adjudged penalties. In the case of the Commodity Exchange Authority, an assistant secretary rather than the administrator signs all complaints.

Conclusions

The wide range of responsibilities of regulatory agencies in these three areas and the significant differences in the nature of their performance indicate that a highly general approach to the problems of regulation is very difficult, if not impossible. The experience with the Department of Agriculture suggests that the structure of the agency probably makes little difference. The critical matter is the nature of the regulatory responsibility and the political balance of power among the interests affected by regulation. If an agency redistributes wealth in an environment in which political power is not in balance, the agency is in continual trouble. A single administrator without tenure of office will be of no help. He will simply lose his position when the balance of political power within the agricultural community shifts. Agency heads, whether single or multiple, need tenure—and preferably a tenure longer than the term of the President or other appointing official. It is also evident in Agriculture that the level of regulatory expertise an administrator brings to his role substantially affects his agency's performance.

CHAPTER SIX

ALLOCATING AGENCY RESOURCES
TO NONLEGAL ISSUES

The Ash Council cites three characteristics of regulation that cause regulatory agencies to devote too few resources to the most important issues of regulation. The first is the multiheaded administrative direction provided by a collegial body, which has been discussed above. The second is the attention to legal arguments and procedures, attributed to the collegial form and the agency review process. The third is the inadequate appropriations given the agencies, said to arise from their independence. The Ash Council proposes new review procedures, the establishment of a federal Administrative Court, and incorporation into the executive branch as means for solving the two latter problems and thereby making more resources available to the nonlegal aspects of regulation.

Reforming Review Procedures

The Ash report claims three major advantages for its proposed reforms of the procedures for reviewing regulatory decisions. First, the status of the first-round decision maker, the hearing examiner, would be enhanced, since more of his decisions would become final agency positions without amendment by the directors of the agency. Second, the agency head (particularly a single administrator) would, with limits imposed on his ability to remand a decision of a hearing examiner, pay more attention to policy and rule making, and less to individual cases. Third, appeals from agency decisions would be heard in a specialized, more expert, less overburdened court, an arrangement that would promote the development of a consistent set of regulatory procedures and facilitate the development of clear legal precedent in regulation.

These all would work to improve the quality of the staffs of agencies and would serve to reduce the relative importance of legal procedures in agency investigations. The focal point of decisions would be the hearing examiner; responsibility for review would be divided into policy review by the head of the regulatory agency and procedural review by the Administrative Court.

Two of the claims made by the Ash Council for this proposal are obviously valid, offering clear advantages over the present system. First, the pressure on the federal court system would be reduced if the roughly 1,200 administrative appeals annually were reassigned to an entirely new court system.[1] Second, the delays associated with the regulatory process would be shortened to the extent that agency heads would review a smaller percentage of the cases decided by hearing examiners. The gains from the latter, however, could be minimal. Agency heads could easily pressure hearing examiners to delay a decision while the agency head decided whether the policy implications of the case would be reviewed. Furthermore, in many agencies in which literally every decision by a hearing examiner must now be formally approved by the commissioners, review is not normally a source of delay because it is perfunctory.[2] To do away with this useless task would save some time and paperwork, but the saving is not likely to be overwhelmingly great.

The prime advantage of the Administrative Court would be its effect on the workload of the federal judicial system. While the need for more federal judges is apparent, the proposal that expansion be accompanied by court specialization is more controversial. One highly pragmatic objection to the proposal is that in the future, as the composition of caseloads in the federal judicial system changes, court specialization could lead to the anomalous situation of an overload in one type of court and too little work in another. A more basic question is whether a specialized Administrative Court is likely to confine itself solely to procedural issues. The line between judicial and legislative functions is blurred, and a court that is assigned only the function of reviewing administrative decisions would, by virtue of its expertise, be strongly tempted to make policy. The present tendency of the federal courts to focus mainly on procedural issues probably has two sources. First, federal

1. Although the Ash Council is not clear on this point, it is assumed that their intention is to give the Administrative Court jurisdiction over all regulatory matters, including appeals from decisions of the regulatory agencies that are not discussed in the report. If this assumption is incorrect the Administrative Court would have very little effect on the caseload of the federal circuit court. Most administrative cases involve the agencies that were not examined by the Ash Council.

2. In the case of the Federal Power Commission, MacAvoy concluded that "the Commissioners more or less automatically granted any application reaching the case level." A "volume of FPC 'decisions of substance' would contain three dozen opinions at most" of the 350-odd decisions reached annually by the Commission. See Paul W. MacAvoy, "The Formal Work-Product of the Federal Power Commissioners," *Bell Journal of Economics and Management Science,* Vol. 2 (Spring 1971), p. 394.

judges do not normally have much knowledge of regulatory problems. Second, the federal courts are too overloaded to afford judges the luxury of policy making in the relatively unimportant regulatory arena.

It is also unrealistic to expect the heads of regulatory agencies to lose interest in procedural matters. The motivation would be strong to avoid having agency decisions overturned in the courts. The administrative head of an agency would still be responsible for decisions, whether he formally reviewed them or not; a procedural error would reflect on the agency generally and the administrative head in particular, as well as the hearing examiner responsible for the error. Furthermore, the distinction between procedure and substance is not clear. The decision to give standing to a particular party in a hearing, or to decide which types of evidence are relevant to a particular case and how the relevant evidence is to be submitted, can significantly affect the outcome of a proceeding. While it is a matter of *procedure* to rule that a party has no standing and a matter of *policy* to decide to give little or no weight to a party that has standing, the effect of the two is the same. One can expect hearing examiners—or, for that matter, judges—who are out of sympathy with agency policy to be especially sensitive to procedural issues that could be used to justify a ruling that is contrary to agency policy.

The Administrative Court would not reduce the attention given by an agency to procedural matters. If anything, the hearing examiner would face an even more careful procedural review of his findings than now is the case. The attention the hearing examiner gives to procedural detail is likely to be governed more by the care with which the review is undertaken than by the number of distinct stages of procedural review. At present, commissioners and federal courts of appeal are less expert on administrative procedures than the Administrative Court presumably would be. Moreover, the Administrative Court would establish procedures to some extent, for example, by encouraging all agencies to adopt a procedural innovation initiated by one. The hearing examiner could then expect an even larger flow of new rules after the court is established.

The proposal really would not make issues other than legal ones more likely to be considered in individual cases, for the role of hearing examiner, while perhaps strengthened, would not be altered. The hearing examiner would have, if anything, less incentive to consult economic and engineering evidence in making his decision, since the likelihood of any review other than a procedural one would be reduced. If the head of an agency were not empowered to overrule the decisions of the hearing examiner on procedural grounds, the problem would be magnified because the hearing examiner could be assured that he could countermand agency policy by finding a procedural loophole. If the agency head could overrule a hearing examiner on procedural as well as on substantive grounds, then the agency head would continue to have a tendency to concentrate on legal issues. Furthermore, in instances where the agency head overruled the examiner on substantive grounds, an examination and decision satisfying the procedural rules would still have to be carried out in the agency to protect against procedural reversal by the courts.

The essential cause of the legalism of regulatory agencies is the requirement that they follow judicial procedures in granting standing, collecting evidence, and making decisions. If the sole test of an administrative decision were only whether the agency had the power to intervene in a particular action, regardless of how arbitrarily the agency behaved in considering the case, the legalism—as well as the protection that legalism provides to regulated parties—would disappear. Administrative procedures are a device to limit the discretionary powers of regulators. They are, to a significant degree, a response to the vagueness and breadth of the legislative mandate that is given to the agencies. Unfortunately they tend to constrain regulation in only one dimension. Administrative procedures are the result of pressures from the legal fraternity to build certain safeguards that protect the property and independence of regulated firms. They do not protect the general public interest, perhaps on the theory that the regulatory agency is supposed to be, in principle, an advocate of the public interest. But as regulation has developed, regulatory agencies have behaved more like neutral, passive judges of the conflict of interests among firms in, or touched by, regulated industry and between the general public and the regulated sector. The procedural safeguards for the regulated firms affect the flow of information to the passive judgmental body, giving that body an impression of the regulatory environment that is overly favorable to the regulated interests. A regulatory authority that attempts to strike the proper balance between public and special interests, but whose information-gathering procedures cause it to receive significantly more and better information favorable to the regulated, will, quite unintentionally, reach decisions that are excessively favorable to the special interests.

The Ash Council proposals do not get to the heart of the legalism problem. The Council assumes that administrative-procedure safeguards are compatible with and separable from objective policy making. The alternative view is that the two are intertwined and are to some degree mutual substitutes. If so, to increase the attention given to nonlegal arguments, policy making, and the general welfare would require some relaxation in the rules of procedure throughout the regulatory process—in the courts and by the hearing examiners as well as by the agency heads.

Increasing Agency Budgets

The proposal to bring regulatory agencies under the wing of the President is intended to have a favorable effect on the budgets of the agencies. First, the agencies would be expected to receive a more responsive hearing within the Office of Management and Budget (OMB). Second, agency heads would be in a better position to appeal the decisions of budget examiners to someone higher in the administration—even to the White House. Third, the President would add more political muscle to the agencies' requests in the Congress.

The premise of the Ash proposal is that agencies are now starved and need substantially larger budgets and staffs. Presumably a substantial change in the resources available to regulatory agencies would produce a substantial change in their performance.

Table 1 shows the budgets and numbers of employees since 1945 of the seven agencies studied by the Ash Council. Over the past twenty-five years regulatory agencies have passed through four distinct periods. The first was a time of rapid growth immediately after the Second World War, in which all the agencies except the Federal Communications Commission (FCC) and the Securities and Exchange Commission (SEC) had substantial increases in both appropriations and employment. Second, beginning around 1950, the agencies entered a period of roughly stable appropriations and declining employment. Third, during the late fifties, another boom in appropriations and employment took place, roughly from 1956 to 1964. Fourth, since about 1964, appropriations have once again become more stable, and employment has declined somewhat. In 1970, all agencies received large budget increases; it remains to be seen whether this is the beginning of a new era or a one-year anomaly.

The Ash report contains several tables similar to Table 1, but they are somewhat misleading as they show only the last of the four periods portrayed here. They give the impression that the agencies have been the victims of long-term neglect, rather than that the past five years have been a readjustment period after the preceding eight-year boom.

The full twenty-five year picture immediately raises two important questions. First, if the independence of the commissions makes them so vulnerable in the budget process, why did they do so well in the first and third periods? The initial boom in agency appropriations after the war was probably due to the relaxation of wartime controls applied to business from elsewhere in the government; as government generally withdrew its administrative controls related to mobilization, the importance of regulatory activities obviously increased. But the boom between 1955 and 1964, when the agencies' appro-

priations tripled and employment increased by 40-100 percent, is more difficult to explain. The boom carried through two administrations, one Republican
and one Democratic, and applied to all agencies.

Second, since the resources available to the agencies increased so dramati-
cally, the performance of the agencies could be expected to have improved to
some extent. In general, the professional literature provides no support for
this view; evaluations of the regulatory agencies are as critical of them now as
in the past. The two exceptions are the Civil Aeronautics Board (CAB) and
the FCC; the former has become distinctly more anticompetitive in recent
years, which most analysts regard as a liability, while in the past few years the
FCC has had a mixed record. The FCC has become somewhat more aggressive
in its attitude toward limiting the dominance of the American Telephone and
Telegraph Company (witness its reversal on the foreign attachments prohibition and its decision to permit competition in private line microwave services)
and slightly tougher in granting broadcast license renewals (as illustrated by
the Lamar Life Broadcasting Company and the WHDH, Inc. cases),[3] but has
steadfastly protected existing television stations against competition (by placing a series of roadblocks in the way of cable television and pay-TV).

If the performance of the agencies did not improve during the late 1950s and
early 1960s, one explanation could be an increase in the demands placed on
them that kept pace with—or outstripped—the increase in their resources. The
Ash Council argues that in fact the responsibilities of the agencies are growing
quite rapidly and cites the recent trends in several measures of agency work-
loads. Table 1 shows the numbers of certain types of cases and the size of the
case backload for several agencies for the years 1945-70[4]—as complete a long-
run picture as can be drawn. A relation between these measures of workload
and resource availability is difficult to perceive. Furthermore, the number of
cases considered is not beyond the control of the agency. Any decision to
expand the regulatory responsibilities of the agency leads to an increased caseload. An increase in resources might lead to better staff work and consequently
better decisions, but it could also lead to an expansion of the regulatory domain
of the agency. If the agency believes that it is operating largely in the public
interest and is not contradicted in that belief by a significant number of rever-
sals in the courts or through negative legislative responses to policies, the agency
is obviously more likely to increase the domain of regulation if the opportunity
should arise, rather than confine itself to performing old duties better.

3. Federal Communications Commission, FCC Dockets 18845-18849, and 8739,
11070, 15204-15207, respectively.
4. These measures are obviously very imperfect. They are used simply because no
reasonable alternative is available and because they were used by the Ash Council.

Table 1. Budget, Personnel, and Workload of Regulatory Agencies Studied by Ash Council, 1945-70

Budget in thousands of dollars

CIVIL AERONAUTICS BOARD[a]

Fiscal year	Budget	Personnel	Workload	
			Processed	Backlog
1945	1,386	343	n.a.	905
1946	1,689	373	n.a.	928
1947	2,382	481	n.a.	1,176
1948	2,982	582	n.a.	933
1949	3,615	668	n.a.	1,010
1950	3,673	653	n.a.	973
1951	3,491	577	830	972
1952	3,784	573	843	969
1953	3,774	574	717	1,011
1954	3,714	538	660	1,088
1955	3,781	537	786	1,164
1956	4,450	569	1,132	1,332
1957	4,651	606	1,402	1,450
1958	5,359	666	1,684	1,616
1959	6,601	703	1,613	1,413
1960	6,832	733	2,129	1,527
1961	7,685	758	2,258	1,316
1962	8,373	790	2,656	1,196
1963	9,374	836	2,297	895
1964	10,023	847	2,203	848
1965	11,205	836	1,906	848
1966	10,856	610	2,022	933
1967	11,536	770	3,270	1,174
1968	9,074	651	4,043	1,349
1969	9,339	654	4,560	991
1970	11,184	658	5,317	998

FEDERAL COMMUNICATIONS COMMISSION[b]

Fiscal year	Budget	Personnel	Workload
1945	6,142	1,520	1,077
1946	5,740	1,404	819
1947	6,170	1,387	1,107
1948	6,137	1,349	1,057
1949	6,621	1,366	785
1950	6,815	1,325	645
1951	6,554	1,239	695
1952	6,547	1,143	1,048
1953	6,798	1,088	830
1954	6,822	1,122	431
1955	6,718	1,039	437
1956	7,564	1,055	527
1957	7,772	1,084	584
1958	8,349	1,098	718
1959	9,920	1,130	864
1960	10,367	1,224	1,042
1961	11,948	1,309	879
1962	13,371	1,346	854
1963	14,088	1,386	667
1964	16,717	1,468	629

See notes at end of table.

Table 1 *(continued)*

FEDERAL COMMUNICATIONS COMMISSION (continued)

Fiscal year	Budget	Personnel	Workload
1965	16,747	1,482	679
1966	17,217	1,465	759
1967	17,965	1,458	752
1968	18,652	1,470	673
1969	20,278	1,458	673
1970	23,368	1,511	n.a.

FEDERAL MARITIME COMMISSION[c]

Fiscal year	Budget	Personnel	Workload	
			New	Backlog
1945	...	...	...	...
1946	...	...	...	...
1947	...	...	...	...
1948	...	...	...	...
1949	...	...	...	...
1950	...	...	...	...
1951	...	...	...	...
1952	...	...	...	...
1953	...	...	...	...
1954	...	...	...	...
1955	...	...	...	...
1956	...	...	...	...
1957	...	...	...	...
1958	...	...	...	...
1959	...	...	...	...
1960	...	...	...	...
1961	...	...	...	...
1962	1,163	188	137	111
1963	2,142	208	70	117
1964	2,611	239	179	60
1965	2,857	240	75	40
1966	3,091	246	52	65
1967	3,454	254	66	73
1968	3,576	253	100	109
1969	3,704	242	50	49
1970	3,947	226	171	94

FEDERAL POWER COMMISSION[d]

Fiscal year	Budget	Personnel
1945	2,645	633
1946	2,900	687
1947	3,735	736
1948	3,763	730
1949	4,236	752
1950	4,130	701
1951	4,149	738
1952	4,288	716
1953	4,257	662
1954	4,286	659
1955	4,201	632
1956	4,982	683
1957	5,204	705
1958	5,572	701

See notes at end of table.

Table 1 *(continued)*

FEDERAL POWER COMMISSION (continued)

Fiscal year	Budget	Personnel
1959	6,967	781
1960	7,207	826
1961	8,003	851
1962	8,786	904
1963	10,712	1,053
1964	12,324	1,115
1965	13,115	1,111
1966	13,402	1,092
1967	14,080	1,131
1968	14,563	1,109
1969	15,666	1,080
1970	17,910	1,095

FEDERAL TRADE COMMISSION[e]

Fiscal year	Budget	Personnel	Workload		Cease and desist orders
			Complaints		
			Total	Textile and fur	
1945	1,910	430	164	n.a.	140
1946	2,130	468	101	n.a.	89
1947	2,825	548	53	n.a.	56
1948	2,960	572	70	n.a.	73
1949	3,492	649	96	5	47
1950	3,745	660	124	11	79
1951	3,765	643	109	22	121
1952	4,253	676	104	5	132
1953	4,215	653	101	13	105
1954	4,195	601	123	16	105
1955	4,048	587	161	42	112
1956	4,590	610	192	46	173
1957	5,406	717	242	72	185
1958	5,917	731	354	112	281
1959	6,687	721	350	125	345
1960	6,750	751	503	89	354
1961	7,854	808	413	115	375
1962	9,562	990	233	91	411
1963	11,515	1,143	431	74	454
1964	12,118	1,155	309	85	385
1965	13,662	1,145	161	69	175
1966	13,648	1,127	194	52	196
1967	14,108	1,119	221	89	215
1968	15,221	1,197	123	62	138
1969	16,402	1,185	220	127	221
1970	19,927	1,302	239	140	230

INTERSTATE COMMERCE COMMISSION[f]

Fiscal year	Budget	Personnel	Workload	
			New	Backlog
1945	8,225	2,017	n.a.	n.a.
1946	8,643	2,058	n.a.	n.a.
1947	10,402	2,240	n.a.	n.a.
1948	10,529	2,248	n.a.	n.a.
1949	11,251	2,218	n.a.	n.a.
1950	11,652	2,161	n.a.	n.a.

See notes at end of table.

Table 1 *(continued)*

INTERSTATE COMMERCE COMMISSION (continued)

Fiscal year	Budget	Personnel	Workload New	Workload Backlog
1951	10,887	2,073	n.a.	n.a.
1952	11,590	1,890	n.a.	n.a.
1953	11,089	1,849	n.a.	n.a.
1954	11,187	1,872	n.a.	n.a.
1955	11,512	1,860	n.a.	n.a.
1956	13,039	1,902	n.a.	n.a.
1957	14,624	2,090	n.a.	n.a.
1958	16,580	2,381	n.a.	n.a.
1959	19,341	2,268	n.a.	n.a.
1960	19,405	2,344	7,195	5,442
1961	22,139	2,386	7,193	5,002
1962	21,971	2,399	7,588	4,688
1963	23,519	2,413	10,655	7,738
1964	24,378	2,411	8,511	6,357
1965	26,491	2,399	9,575	5,993
1966	27,264	1,953	11,572	8,050
1967	27,107	1,929	7,677	6,108
1968	23,706	1,899	7,465	5,264
1969	24,582	1,802	7,508	4,962
1970	27,464	1,802	8,334	5,332

SECURITIES AND EXCHANGE COMMISSION [g]

Fiscal year	Budget	Personnel	Workload Registration statements	Workload Proxy statements
1945	4,241	1,141	340	1,594
1946	4,727	1,173	661	1,685
1947	5,493	1,187	493	1,645
1948	5,532	1,160	435	1,677
1949	6,083	1,156	429	1,653
1950	5,891	1,062	487	1,668
1951	5,929	1,040	487	1,788
1952	5,580	930	635	1,818
1953	5,459	813	593	1,817
1954	4,964	750	631	1,860
1955	4,774	692	779	1,887
1956	5,211	704	906	2,016
1957	5,765	783	876	1,991
1958	6,491	840	813	1,929
1959	7,898	910	1,070	1,975
1960	8,126	952	1,426	2,089
1961	9,331	1,030	1,550	2,197
1962	10,988	1,180	1,844	2,259
1963	13,207	1,378	1,157	2,396
1964	14,337	1,383	1,121	2,530
1965	15,276	1,393	1,266	2,661
1966	15,820	1,372	1,523	4,109
1967	16,681	1,360	1,649	4,633
1968	17,642	1,370	2,147	5,224
1969	18,550	1,317	3,645	5,316
1970	21,513	1,388	n.a.	n.a.

Sources: President's Advisory Council on Executive Organization, *A New Regulatory Framework: Report on Selected Independent Regulatory Agencies* (1971), pp. 145, 146, 152, 153, 170, 172, 178, 186, 187, for 1965-69 data. U.S. Department of the Treasury,

An interesting feature of Table 1 is the steady increase in cases that has occurred in most agencies since the return to stable budgets. The Ash report conclusions on understaffing in the agencies would be clearly evident if the situation in regulated industries had deteriorated significantly since the mid-1960s. In the CAB, employment has fallen 20 percent since 1965, while the caseload has more than doubled. Yet the backlog of cases, after a brief period of sharp increase, has declined. By contrast, the backlog was highest during the boom period. At the Interstate Commerce Commission (ICC) employment has declined 25 percent since 1965, but the backlog has also fallen sharply. While employment in the Federal Trade Commission (FTC) has remained constant since 1963 (except for a sharp increase in 1970), the number of cases has fallen by half—and by more than half outside of the textile and fur enforcement category, where the number of cases has actually risen.

The Ash Council concludes that the decline in employment and the relatively constant budgets that have occurred since 1965 are a consequence of the independent status of the commissions. An alternative hypothesis that appears more consistent with the historical data is that regulatory agencies were given their chance during the late 1950s and early 1960s, that they responded to the increased budgets and employment levels granted them by expanding their regulatory domain rather than by improving their performance, and that the budgeters in the Congress and the executive reacted to this by cutting back support for the agencies.

In response to an informal, unscientific survey, the impressions of several officials of the Bureau of the Budget (now OMB) during the mid-1960s on how the budgets of regulatory agencies were handled was consistent with the

---

Notes to Table 1 (continued)
Combined Statement of Receipts, Expenditures and Balances of the United States Government; The Budget of the United States Government—Appendix; and agency files and annual reports, for 1945-64 and 1970 data.

n.a. Not available.

a. Budget figures do not include subsidies. Workload measures the number of economic enforcement cases docketed or on file with CAB during each year.

b. Workload measures the number of broadcasting station applications pending each year; figures for 1945-48 are approximations for all stations, and for 1949-70 for commercial stations only.

c. Established in 1961. Workload measures the number of proceedings before the FMC each year; the basis for counting backlog varied in 1965, but is comparable to 70 proceedings in other years.

d. The Ash Council did not measure the workload of the FPC.

e. Budget includes payments to states under permanent appropriations. Workload measures number of complaints and cease and desist orders issued by the FTC.

f. Workload measures the number of proceedings handled; the basis for counting backlog varied after 1964 but is comparable to 69 and 70 proceedings in earlier years. Before 1960, ICC data were reported for calendar year under a somewhat different system.

g. Workload measures the numbers of registration statements (proposals to offer securities to the public) and proxy statements (solicitations of proxies from stockholders), which companies must file with the SEC.

latter hypothesis. In general, the budgets of the regulatory agencies were not examined closely at the higher levels of the Bureau, partly because the budgets were small and partly because of a general feeling that the agencies were not effective. The exception occurred when an exciting new commissioner—particularly a chairman—was appointed to an agency. There was then a tendency to give the new man a little financial elbow room to see what he could do with the agency. (Perhaps the 1970 budget increases in the first budget year of the Nixon administration were made for similar reasons—to support the new chairmen installed by the new President.) When the war in Vietnam began to squeeze the overall budget, the regulatory agencies were a prime target for pruning. In fact, these were among the few wartime budget cuts that were made without serious objections from within the executive office of the President.

While the historical evidence does not lend support to the view that regulation could be improved if only the budgets of the agencies were larger,[5] it is consistent with a more important point made by the Ash Council—that fundamental changes are needed to make regulation work effectively. Although the changes required might be something other than the organizational reforms proposed in the Ash report, nevertheless a revolutionary change appears necessary to achieve significant results.

Summary on Agency Resources

The Ash Council contends that reorganizing regulatory agencies would make regulation more effective by providing agencies with a greater number and better allocation of resources. The argument advanced here is that the creation of an Administrative Court, the transfer of the agencies to the executive branch, and the limitations placed on case review by agency administrators are all unlikely to have much of an effect on agency performance. The historical record provides ample reason to believe that agencies would probably continue to be legalistic and formal, and to spend budget increases on expanding the domain of regulation rather than on improving the quality of regulation in the areas already regulated.

5. One could still hold that the budget increases of the boom period were small compared to the need—that an enormous increase in support would achieve effective regulation. The evidence does not refute this view; however, with the budget for these seven regulatory agencies now totaling around $125 million, and with about fifty more regulatory authorities scattered throughout the government that function roughly as ineffectively as do the seven under discussion, the costs of effective administrative control are astronomical even if this view is correct. These costs would cast grave doubt on whether most regulation is worth undertaking.

CHAPTER SEVEN

PROPOSALS FOR REFORM

During the past few years, several proposals have been advanced for improving the performance of regulatory agencies. Some important recommendations are not mentioned in the Ash report,[1] primarily because they often touch on the problem of defining the proper scope of regulation—an issue that the Ash Council did not regard as within its legitimate area of concern. This chapter is devoted to a review of a few of these proposals.

The Regulatory Czar

The idea that all regulatory activities ought to be under the general direction of a single member of the President's administration has gone through several reincarnations. Perhaps the most publicized is Rexford Tugwell's proposal that the Constitution be amended to place the responsibility for all regulation in the hands of a single official—a second vice president. In 1960, James Landis proposed that a member of the White House staff be given the authority to oversee the regulatory agencies.[2]

These proposals go one step beyond the Ash Council recommendations, which would retain the separate status of the regulatory agencies by having each report directly to the President. Nevertheless, the arguments used to defend the "czar" proposals are similar to those used by the Ash Council. A single regulatory czar would be more visible politically and would be given more serious attention by the general public, the Congress, and the White House. He would be more able to fight for agency policy, new legislation, and bigger budgets. Coordination no longer would be problematical, but would

1. The appendixes to the Ash report summarize several proposals of past government and private commissions that are not discussed here, nor are they discussed in any detail in the body of the Ash report.

2. See *New York Times,* Sept. 8, 1970, and James M. Landis, *Report on Regulatory Agencies to the President-Elect* (1960).

flow automatically from a single, responsible source. Finally, regulatory policy as one of the President's responsibilities would be more subject to the position-trading discussed in Chapter 4.

Since the "regulatory czar" proposal would go even further in the direction the Ash Council favors, it is surprising that the Council did not even discuss it in the report. (Certainly the profusion of references to Landis in the Ash report indicates that the Council was aware of the proposal.)

Perhaps the answer lies in the congressional reaction to the Landis report in 1961. The attitude of congressmen was expressed by Senator McClellan: "I think the concern is this, and I share it to some extent, that we want to keep these boards or commissions independent. Nobody wants them to get under the domination of the President, or the assistant to the President, or somebody else."[3] The Ash report steps back from the regulatory czar proposal and recommends a profusion of agencies (as now), but proposes that they be incorporated into the executive branch. Senator McClellan's further remarks bring even the feasibility of the Ash proposal into question: "We want to keep them independent . . . and not . . . under the executive branch of the Government."

The principal merit of the proposal, beyond the reasons shared with the Ash report recommendations, is that it might be the only mechanism for elevating regulatory policy to an important general political issue. Given the ever increasing scope and complexity of government, it is increasingly unlikely that the policy issues of a specific regulatory agency will ever capture more than temporary general public attention. A single regulatory official would be a vehicle for building more generalized regulatory issues. In addition, as a single source of news about regulation, the official would capture more publicity for these issues. Just as news agencies find it worthwhile to keep in touch with cabinet officials and heads of important offices, they might find a single regulatory czar sufficiently newsworthy to justify regular surveillance. (Regulatory agencies are not covered carefully by the press.)

The principal disadvantage of the proposal is its inherent potential for disaster. An administration elected on issues that are unrelated to regulation not only could promulgate regulatory policies that were uniformly disastrous, but could also coordinate its disastrous policies effectively. Nevertheless, the incremental danger of the czar proposal over the Ash proposal does not seem great: once the regulatory agencies crawl inside the executive branch, the

3. Hearings on Reorganization Plans of 1961 before the Senate Committee on Government Operations, June 6, 1961, as quoted in William L. Cary, *Politics and the Regulatory Agencies* (McGraw-Hill, 1967), p. 29.

danger of destructive presidential leadership will have been accepted. The issue here is only a slightly altered version of the traditional debate over independence versus political control.

Legislative Reform

Another approach, following the critique of Friendly[4] and Lowi,[5] would be to rewrite the administrative laws in a manner that limits the authority and clarifies the policy objectives of regulatory agencies. For example, the national transportation goals contained in the Transportation Act of 1920, many of which are mutually inconsistent, would be replaced by clear statements about the purpose of price regulation, the extent of cross-subsidization that is in the national interest, the factors that should be considered in awarding franchises and licenses, and the appropriate role of competition.

A second legislative reform that is worth considering is to undo at least part of the Administrative Procedure Act, eliminating many of the formal procedural requirements that are imposed on regulatory agencies. Several procedural precedents other than the judicial would be suitable. For example, grant-giving agencies, such as the National Science Foundation or the Office of Economic Opportunity, are not encumbered with complicated rules on how to make their decisions, even though they give away wealth "in the public interest" to competing parties.[6]

A variant of the legislative reform approach is the proposal to deregulate many types of business behavior on the grounds that regulation now serves to prevent workable competition in areas where competition would be beneficial. In some cases an entire industry might be deregulated—for example, surface freight transportation. In other instances regulation might apply only to the parts of an industry in which competition is not effective. In the case of commercial airlines, major trunk routes might be opened to competition, while regulation of the less dense routes and feeder lines might continue. In short, regulation would be limited to consumer protection and control of noncompetitive markets; cartelization of a regulated industry, for whatever reason (including cross-subsidization), would not be included as a regulatory responsibility.

4. Henry J. Friendly, *The Federal Administrative Agencies: The Need for Better Definition of Standards* (Harvard University Press, 1962).

5. Theodore Lowi, *The End of Liberalism: Ideology, Policy, and the Crisis of Public Authority* (Norton, 1969).

6. Administrative procedures can, of course, be too lax. Consider, for example, the differences in the protection of regulated firms in regulatory matters and of the poor in the welfare system!

A final legislative reform would be to nationalize certain industries in which social welfare losses would be unreasonable if the industry were left alone by government. Regulatory agencies would either become, or be replaced by, directors of a government enterprise. Of course, nationalization is an emotional issue in the United States. It is generally regarded as a last resort in a hopelessly desperate situation. Two examples are the Tennessee Valley Authority in the depression and Amtrak today, when railroad passenger service is on the verge of collapse. Yet if one accepts the view that limited managerial control through regulation is inherently inefficient, one is forced to choose among admittedly unattractive alternatives—(1) the status quo of more or less weak regulation; (2) widespread deregulation, which would in some cases lead to monopolistic abuse, inefficiently low product quality, and inadequate attention to secondary effects of products and production techniques; or (3) nationalization. In cases where the first two approaches would yield seriously deficient performance, nationalization is surely worthy of dispassionate study.

Independence with Presidential Policy Oversight

Since the major difficulty with regulation, according to the Ash Council, is the failure of the agencies to make clear, coherent policy (a criticism similar to that made by Friendly and Lowi), a possible solution—less radical than the others—would be to create through legislation a new class of executive orders that would pertain to the regulatory agencies. Under this proposal the President would be given the power to make general regulatory rules and policies (not to decide specific cases) by issuing an executive order. To allay the fears of the Congress, the executive order would take effect only if neither the Senate nor the House voted to countermand the order within a specified time period.

To some extent, regulatory agencies already are subject to executive orders. Recent court decisions have required that regulatory agencies follow presidential directives to consider environmental issues in regulatory matters. But the President does not have the power to make regulatory policy, either generally ("The CAB should, wherever viable competition is possible, deregulate airlines with respect to both prices and route awards") or specifically ("The New York-Washington route has sufficient traffic to warrant deregulation").

Safeguards would have to be built into the executive order authority to prevent interference in particular cases, such as by "Louis B. Mayer clauses"[7]

7. See "Ah, To Be Louis B. Mayer," Chapter 3 in Philip M. Stern, *The Great Treasury Raid* (Random House, 1962).

("Henceforth all routes between points in Texas and California shall be awarded to airlines flying proud birds with golden tails"). To some degree the veto power of the Congress would protect against this; another safeguard would be to exclude from the domain of executive orders issues relating to the choice among contending parties in a pending case; still another safeguard is the open, public nature of executive orders.

Presidential policy-making power of this type is not likely to be used to excess, for the responsibilities of the President are too overwhelming to permit him to devote much effort, attention, or political capital to regulation. Furthermore, the fundamental independence of the commissions that many believe to be desirable would be maintained. A major failing of the agencies—their difficulty in making policy—would to some extent be overcome by transferring some of the responsibility to the office most able to make policy decisions.

The Planning Requirement

Probably the most significant achievements of regulation during the past decade have resulted from a handful of in-depth studies of regulatory problems. The FPC National Power Survey of 1964, the SEC Special Study of the Securities Markets completed in 1963, and the 1971 FCC study of broadcast license renewals all were planning studies with important implications for regulatory policy.[8] The first two studies have been credited with making major contributions to policy in the relevant agencies, and thereby with having been responsible for several beneficial changes in the operation of the regulated industries. The FCC study of license renewals may lead to considerably greater specificity in the requirements for license renewal and more citizen participation in renewal proceedings.

With these few exceptions, regulatory agencies have shown little inclination to make—or to welcome when performed by others—broad evaluations of industry and regulatory agency performance. Congressional committees have shown even less interest.

Friendly has made two proposals for promoting long-term planning and better policy definition.[9] First, regulatory agencies should be required to make periodic, systematic studies of each of their major responsibilities. The studies should contain specific statements about the policy of the agency

8. See *National Power Survey,* A Report by the Federal Power Commission, 1964 (Government Printing Office, 1964); "The Special Study," in Cary, *Politics and the Regulatory Agencies,* pp. 71-79; and "A Lurch Toward Tighter Program Control," in *Broadcasting,* Vol. 80 (Feb. 22, 1971), pp. 28-30.
9. Friendly, *The Federal Administrative Agencies,* pp. 145-46.

pertaining to the responsibility being examined. Second, perhaps once a decade the relevant congressional subcommittee should be required to review all of the laws applying to a particular regulatory agency. This proposal is only one step short of the recommendation that all administrative laws should have expiration dates.

The principal argument against the proposal is that it would be ineffective. In the past, in-depth studies have been effective because they have arisen spontaneously from a perception by the regulators, the regulated, and the Congress that a particular issue needed evaluation. The chance that a study will affect policy is slim enough when the subject of the study *requests* it, as is illustrated by the low success rate of presidential advisory commissions. When the study is *required*—forced on the subject—the chances that it will be good (will the agency cooperate, and will a competent group be found to carry out the study?) and that the agency will pay attention to the completed product are both small. (Of course, there is a limit to how uncooperative and unresponsive to constructive evaluation an agency can be without causing a legislative response.)

The proposal does attack, considerably more directly, two related problems cited by the Ash Council. One is the lack of attention to nonlegal issues, the other is the failure to develop coherent policy, particularly with respect to a new technology or other innovation, before it becomes a specific issue in a case before the agency. The Ash Council sought a mechanism that would result in more agency resources being devoted to planning and substantive policy analysis; it proposed to reduce the legal orientation of agencies and to encourage more receptivity to agency budget requests (the topics of Chapter 6). The Friendly proposal is more direct—to require that the agencies, and the legislative oversight subcommittees, engage in these activities.

Commissions of Constituent Representatives

One possible way to broaden the range of views represented in a regulatory commission would be to allot each position on a regulatory commission to a representative of a particular interest. Some positions on the commission would be formally reserved for employees on leave from regulated firms; other positions would be reserved for representatives of other groups, with, of course, no single group given enough representatives to control the commission.

The positions that make up the set of alternative policies considered by a regulatory agency are determined in part by the interest groups mobilized to present their case to the agency and, if a decision is unacceptable, to appeal the decision outside the agency. The other limiting factor to the range of alternatives considered is the predisposition of the commissioners.

In a regulatory agency, the median policy position after all groups have had their say is likely to be closer to the industry point of view than is socially desirable. Neither in lobbying before the commission, in threatening to appeal outside the commission, nor in pressing for sympathetic appointees does the general public or a consumer interest have representation commensurate with its total stake in the issue.

The "constituent representative" proposal formally recognizes the reality of interest-group influence in appointments to commissions. It attempts to move the median position within the regulatory commission closer to the societal median by expanding representation on the commission. The presumption is that the Congress, while incapable of specifying policy objectives to regulators, can structure the representation on a commission to achieve broadly representative policy.

The constituent representation method of organizing a commission is relatively common in one important area of government regulation—pollution abatement and control, particularly watershed management. Typically, a commission organized to reduce pollution in a given area formally has positions reserved for representatives of polluting industries, all levels of government, and conservation groups.[10]

The main liability of the constituent representation collegial body is the difficulty it is likely to have in reaching decisions. A commission would have to find a compromise among even more divergent interests than are now represented, yet even now regulatory commissions are notoriously slow in making decisions. To be effective, a constituent body would have to be subject to time limits in deciding a case.

10. For an interesting analysis of how such constituent representation commissions operate, see Edwin T. Haefele, "Environmental Quality as a Problem of Social Choice," in Allen V. Kneese and Blair Bower (eds.), *Environmental Quality Analysis: Studies in the Social Sciences* (to be published by Johns Hopkins Press for Resources for the Future); and Robert Dorfman and Henry D. Jacoby, "A Model of Public Decisions Illustrated by a Water Pollution Policy Problem," in Robert H. Haveman and Julius Margolis (eds.), *Public Expenditures and Policy Analysis* (Markham, 1970).

CHAPTER EIGHT

THE BROOKINGS CONFERENCE
ON REFORMING REGULATION

A panel of thirty-two experts on government regulation met at the Brookings Institution on April 8, 1971, to discuss the Ash report proposals and related issues. An earlier draft of the preceding chapters served as a background paper for the conference.

In attendance at the conference were lawyers, political scientists, and economists, many with considerable experience as government officials in regulatory agencies or in policy-making positions within the executive office of the President.[1] The conference was not designed to produce a uniform, coherent, expert view on the Ash report or on regulation generally. Diversity, rather than consensus, was actively sought so that a full range of critiques of regulation and reform proposals could be considered. The following summary of the conference proceedings does not represent a consensus of the conferees, but rather contains the points made during the conference discussion that, in the author's judgment, were the most interesting and provocative, together with assessments of the apparent extent of agreement on the major issues discussed. Although the conferees were often in substantial agreement, on nearly all issues some participants disagreed strongly with the majority view; few if any found themselves always in agreement with the majority. Consequently no participant should be held accountable for the majority viewpoints summarized below.

Separating Structure from Substance

The Ash report was written on the assumption that the choice of policy objectives could largely be separated from the choice of an effective organizational structure. A few conferees offered some defense for this position. They

---

1. See Appendix B for a list of the participants.

argued that the principal problem of most regulation is to strike a proper balance between operational effectiveness and fairness to the affected parties. One conferee went so far as to argue that discussion about the proper direction of policy—including consideration of economic issues—is largely irrelevant to the issue of reforming the organizational structure of regulation, the latter being the domain of lawyers and political scientists.

The great majority of the conference participants rejected this view on the grounds that it is appropriate to ask first whether different organizational arrangements can be expected to produce significantly different policies from the same legislative mandate and second whether any organizational structure can be expected to carry out effectively certain types of mandates. The proposals of the Ash Council could then be evaluated at least in part on the basis of the changes in regulatory policy that are likely to flow from them.

As one conferee pointed out, in a few instances the legislation establishing a regulatory function contains policy directions that are highly controversial. The Robinson-Patman Act and the mandate to regulate trucking are prime examples. In these cases the separation of policy issues from the choice of an organizational structure is valid, since the complaint about the performance of the regulated sector is not entirely that a regulatory agency has made a socially undesirable interpretation of a vague law. Yet in the view of most conference participants, the principal point of controversy regarding policy is the interpretation that agencies have given to legislation. If the internal structure of an agency and the position of the agency within the governmental hierarchy can lead to certain policy predispositions, organizational and policy issues cannot be separated. As one conferee expressed the majority view:

> If the agencies had, with fair uniformity over the years, established sensible, workable, progressive policies, we would not much care how they arrived at these policies. The clearest proof that the agencies are not working is that their policies are not clear, progressive, efficient, or workable. The present machinery, quite apart from the elements of due process, simply has not produced satisfactory results.

The Problems of Regulation

After accepting the issue as relevant, the conferees turned to evaluating the regulatory policies as a preliminary step toward discussing whether the Ash Council proposals would improve the performance of the agencies. The economists predictably voiced the opinion that the main criticism of regulation is that it sacrifices economic efficiency. First, public utility regulation does not succeed in controlling prices except insofar as it occasionally protects administered pricing in the face of incipient competition. Thus the initial objective of regulation, which was to eliminate the worst abuses of monopoly pricing, has not been achieved.[2] Second, the principal devices used to prevent monopoly prices from creating monopoly profits are the imposition of expensive regulatory rules and the requirement to provide uneconomic service. One participant estimated that regulated firms may spend as much as a billion dollars a year dealing with government regulatory agencies; another remarked that regulation has become, more than anything else, a full employment program for lawyers. Third, agencies with responsibilities for promoting competition are too passive and pay too little attention to the economic consequences of anticompetitive behavior. Fourth, agencies with mandates to promote product quality and truthful information about products do not enforce high enough standards.

The economists' evaluation of regulation was criticized on two grounds. First, the economists were accused of comparing the performance of regulated industries to the hypothesized performance of an idealized, unrealistic model—perfect competition. In most regulated industries, competition is impossible. The relevant comparison is with other forms of regulation or with unregulated monopoly. The defenders of economic efficiency responded that one purpose of regulation is to do as good a job as possible in simulating competition in sectors where true competition is not possible. To the extent that regulation produces monopoly prices, high enforcement costs, and uneconomic services, it may be even more inefficient than unregulated monopoly. Furthermore, the same evidence that supports the argument that regulation produces inefficient pricing and uneconomic service could be used as the basis for better pricing and more rational provision of service, if regulatory agencies would use that evidence both in making policy and in deciding individual cases. Finally, public utility regulation has tended to take a single approach—imposing governmental controls on price, investment, and entry decisions whether the regulated industry is monopolistic, oligopolistic, or competitive.

The second major criticism of the economic efficiency argument was that economic efficiency may not be a desideratum of the general public. As one conferee put it,

A procedure could be regarded as successful if it is responsive to a majority will expressed through the Congress and/or the President, even if it contravenes every doctrine that economists propound. A political scientist can say

2. A clear exception to this generalization, discussed at some length at the conference, is the regulation of natural gas field prices. Here prices are kept artificially low; at current prices, excess demand is substantial. Of course, limiting supply by keeping prices too low is as inefficient as permitting monopoly prices that are far above incremental costs.

that the system is working perfectly, though it produces idiotic decisions from an economic point of view, as long as it satisfies the principal value of representativeness.

Two responses were made to this point. First, political choice is highly sensitive to the content of political debate. Most professional students of regulation believe that a principal failure of regulation is that it preserves or creates economic inefficiency. There is no reason to suppose that the electorate, given the opportunity to cast a vote solely on the issue of government regulation after a full public debate, would not arrive at the same conclusion. Second, the fact that the Congress has failed to rewrite the regulatory mandate despite forty years of professional criticism is not evidence that the general public does not favor regulatory reform. In the words of one conferee, "The burden on the Congress to undo something is enormously heavier, especially as the something is smaller and smaller." Not the least of the problems involved in changing regulatory policy through congressional action is that every regulatory function is associated with two congressional subcommittees that owe much of their importance and power to the interest created by the existing regulatory mandate. A congressional mandate is likely to be more representative of the general public interest than pressure—usually nonstatutory and informal—exerted by a subcommittee chairman, although, obviously, the subcommittee has an important influence on any legislation passed by Congress.

Most conferees accepted the view that economic efficiency ought to be the principal objective of regulation. For regulators consciously to scorn policies that are consistent with their legislative mandate and that would improve efficiency constitutes a serious indictment of regulation. Furthermore, if the primary objective of a policy is to protect a regulated firm or industry rather than consumers of the service or the general public, the presumption is strong that the policy is ill conceived.

Responsiveness to the Regulated

The conferees generally regarded the tendency of regulators to be too responsive to the interests of regulated industries as the main cause of undesirable regulatory policies and industry performance. This does not mean that regulators are necessarily passive conduits for industry interests. The dissatisfaction of regulated firms with regulation is inconsistent with that notion. It means rather that regulatory agencies, in striking some sort of "balance" between the regulated industry and the general public, persistently assign too much weight to the interests of the former. The principal explanation for this tendency offered at the conference was the environment in which regulation operates. Specifically, most of the information and external contacts of the agency are supplied by the regulated industry. One conferee expressed the problem in the form of a parable about "the care and feeding of regulators."

It all begins when a fellow out in Indianapolis is designated to be a member of a regulatory commission. First he gets into the going-away period. There are banquets in his honor, and the women say to his wife, "For goodness' sake, be sure to tell us what Pat is really like." She demurely replies, "I am sure I won't see her often," believing, of course, that she will. After the goodbyes, the fellow comes to Washington and assumes his role as a member of a commission, believing that he is really a pretty important guy. After all, he almost got elected to Congress back home in Indiana. He is used to public attention. But after a few weeks in Washington, he realizes that nobody ever heard of him or cares much what he does—except one group of very personable, reasonable, knowledgeable, delightful human beings, who recognize his true worth. Obviously, they might turn his head just a bit.

A related problem mentioned by several conferees is the quality of appointments to the regulatory agencies. Presumably the theory of the regulatory commission is based on a faith in expertise and good judgment. The problems facing the commissions involve complex technical, economic, and engineering issues that few regulators can comprehend. Yet, as the demands made upon decision makers have increased, appointments have remained largely political payoffs, primarily to lawyers with little or no experience with the industry being regulated. To come to grips with the issues facing him, a regulator must not only learn the facts about the regulated industry, but must educate himself in several highly technical disciplines as well. Most regulators do not make this effort, preferring to act as passive judges, responding to technically watered-down arguments placed before them. Given the resources of the regulated industries, it is not surprising that their side of a controversy usually appears reasonable—particularly in the vast majority of instances in which they have no organized opposition.

While no disagreement was voiced with the preceding characterization of the qualifications and behavior of agencies, some conferees disputed the conclusion that the solution is to appoint smarter commissioners and to spend more money on staff. These conferees offered several arguments to support their view. First, since in their opinion commissioners are, in general, as able as other executive appointees, there is a serious question as to how much better the appointments to commissions could be. Second, regulatory agencies may never be a match for industry in any event. Presumably an increase in the competence of the regulatory agencies would, to some degree at least, be matched by the regulated firms. Perhaps it is unrealistic to expect regulatory agencies ever to command resources comparable to the professional manpower at the disposal of the regulated industry. Some regulated industries and even a few individual firms already spend many times as much in presenting their cases before regulatory agencies as the agencies spend in investigating the cases. If the regulatory agency does not have commissioners and staff that are comparable in quality and quantity to their counterparts in industry, the only hope for regulation is either to make regulatory mandates and procedures foolproof, or to change the constituency of the agency so that groups other than the regulated industry are effectively represented.

Vagueness in Policies

The conference participants generally agreed that the lack of clarity in regulatory policies creates a critical problem. First, the Congress has not seen fit to write legislation with specific policy mandates, preferring fatuous, self-contradictory wish-lists such as the National Transportation Policy section of the Transportation Act of 1940.[3] Second, the agencies have not stated broad, general policies, but have instead adopted the practice of letting policies develop implicitly through a series of decisions on related specific cases. Third, the courts have not attempted to state policy justifications for specific decisions, nor have they forced the agencies to follow precedent.

Many conferees expressed skepticism that the Congress could be induced to make regulatory legislation more specific. Vague legislation contains less political dynamite and requires less depth of knowledge about the problems of regulation. As one discussant put it, "When Congress delegates with uncertainty and vagueness, it is largely because Congress is incapable of doing anything more on these kinds of problems."

One conferee saw the judicial system as both a primary cause of the problem of vagueness and the main hope for greater clarity. In his judgment, the courts are the institutions most able to require a clearer specification of policy.

The courts have spun some nondelegation doctrine that the legislative body is required to state meaningful standards to administrators. That doctrine has failed completely. But the push to get clarification of policies is a sound one. We are just over the brink of solving this problem for the first time. The solution lies in judicially enforced requirements that administrators use rule-making power to clarify standards, principles, and rules as rapidly as is feasible. Several courts have rendered clear-cut decisions to that effect so far. On January 7, 1971, the D.C. Circuit Court said that we were on the threshhold of a new era, and later, in the second such case before it, said there is a powerful new trend in the law. This is unusual judicial language.

There was general agreement that the courts have a special responsibility to require regulatory agencies to make policy clear. The courts are more

3. 54 Stat. 899.

insulated from special interest pressures than are either the regulatory agencies or the Congress and can be expected to have less reason for countenancing vagueness. Consequently judges might be responsive to appeals from other professionals that the courts be more active in insisting on clearer policy statements from the agencies.

The Ash Council Proposals

The conferees discussed in some detail most of the Ash Council proposals: a single administrator, reorganization into the executive, the Administrative Court, limits on review of hearing examiner decisions, combining the transportation regulatory agencies, and breaking up the Federal Trade Commission. On each issue only a few conferees supported the Ash Council recommendations.

Single Administrator versus Collegial Body

While a few conferees thought that there were some advantages in placing a single administrator in charge of regulatory agencies, no one contended, as did the Ash Council, that this reform would profoundly affect the quality and effectiveness of regulation. The proponents saw two principal benefits of the proposal: more expeditious procedures and better appointees (because they would be less likely to be regarded as representing particular regulatory constituencies). The conferees agreed that most of the problems of regulation would remain even with a single administrator. Regulated industries would still expect to have some influence in appointments, and the agency would still be beholden to a particular congressional subcommittee chairman. Furthermore, the potential for disaster resulting from one bad appointment would increase significantly.

One conferee suggested that collegial bodies have a significant advantage over agencies run by a single administrator: collegial bodies offer the possibility of a dissenting voice at the highest level of policy making. In regulatory agencies, as in the Supreme Court, a well-argued dissenting opinion occasionally becomes more important in the long run than an ill-founded majority opinion. A commissioner who is out of sympathy with a policy adopted by the agency has access to agency data and staff so that his dissent can be based on the best available information. The fact that a disgruntled member can "blow the whistle" on an incompetent or dishonest majority can be important in shaping agency decisions and arousing public opinion on an important regulatory issue.

Another conferee suggested that adequate use has not been made of the potential in the collegial structure for having a diversity of technical sophistication at the highest policy-making level. The Ash Council proposal for placing two economists on the three-man federal antitrust board won high marks from this discussant; indeed, he would go further and insist that economists, engineers, and perhaps political scientists, as well as lawyers, politicians, and businessmen, be represented on commissions. Implicit in this argument is the view that collegial bodies are too much like agencies run by a single administrator in that, except perhaps for political affiliation, they are too homogeneous.

Independence or Executive Control

The conferees were unanimous in believing that independence is desirable for at least some types of regulatory decisions, if for no other reason than the credibility it gives to the agencies' objectivity. The conferees agreed that the "independence" of the existing independent agencies is to some degree illusory. The agencies are subject to congressional and executive pressures, partly because of the budgetary control exercised in these branches and partly because the President and the Congress are elected and therefore deservedly capture the attention of the regulators. Nevertheless, regulators do need the authority to make decisions that are contrary to the wishes of the other branches. This forces the offended branch to make a public show of reversing the agency through new legislation, rather than allowing the exercise of congressional or executive will to be surreptitious. The necessary institutional ingredient for independent decision making is a long-term tenured appointment, which, regardless of the rhetoric or the organization charts, accounts for all of whatever independence the independent agencies enjoy.

Many conferees pointed out that incompetence and/or excessive sensitivity to regulated firms are as common within the executive as in independent agencies. Every agency, particularly the smaller ones, must develop a constituency to give it some power with the politicians. Most often the only candidate for this role is the industry that the agency controls or subsidizes. Particularly when agencies are responsible for making decisions that affect the distribution of wealth between the general public and the regulated industry, all agencies, no matter where they are located, are subject to strong pressures to bend to the interests of the regulated industry, since the latter is likely to be the only potential source of political support for the agency.

The Administrative Court

Through the establishment of an Administrative Court, the Ash Council seeks to separate "policy making" from "procedure." The conferees generally agreed that such a separation would be both undesirable and unattainable. The judicial system obviously has a responsibility to determine whether an agency policy is consistent with the agency's legislative mandate. Furthermore, the interpretation of an agency decision, a procedural rule, or a legislative mandate is made ultimately by the courts and has important policy overtones. In short, as one conferee put it, "There ain't going to be any such animal that can review procedure only and leave substance alone." Since some provision for substantive review must be made, the end result is likely to be either a system much like the one that now exists, constituting in essence an expansion of the Circuit Courts of Appeals, or a new layer of judicial review, which will cause new delays.

Assuming that an Administrative Court would deal with substantive policy issues, the conferees were divided on the value of a specialized court. Some argued that an expansion of the Circuit Courts of Appeals is preferable, partly because of the general overload on these courts (little of which is accounted for by administrative cases) and partly because of past unsatisfactory experience with specialized courts, such as the Commerce Court which, between 1910 and 1913, reviewed decisions of the Interstate Commerce Commission. Furthermore, because existing courts have recently made a flurry of beneficial decisions in administrative cases, the time is not propitious for a legislative change that implies disapproval of current court practices and policies.

Proponents of the specialized court contend that it offers an opportunity for infusing specialized knowledge, particularly of economics, into the review of agency decisions. For example, an expert court would expect an agency to explain the basis for a decision contrary to all of the independent expert advice and analysis on the issue. Opponents of the specialized court argued that the review court is the wrong stage of the decision process at which to infuse specialized knowledge; proponents responded that it might be easier to get qualified experts to serve as judges on a general administrative court than on a single agency. The opponents also suggested that regulated industries would try to influence appointments to the court, raising an important issue of possible capture of the court by the regulated.

One conferee summarized the discussion as follows:

The theory of the present system of "generalist" courts is that judicial review serves as a "window to the outside world." Having a generalist look at the work of the specialist is a way to alleviate some of the problems of regulation, such as an agency's preoccupation with its own interest groups and past history. Most lawyers think that the present system operates well. The other model for judicial review is that of the specialist court. It is based on the view that in regulatory matters you need lawyers with training in economics or economists with training in the law to look at these complicated questions. A concern about this model, with which we have had less experience, is that appointees might be of a lower caliber, especially if the jurisdiction of the court is confined to a few agencies. Appointees might turn out to be industry people—for example, people whose careers had been exclusively in surface transportation. This would just transfer the captive-agency problem to the courts. The old-fashioned administrative court proposals would have given the court jurisdiction over issues touching a broad range of American business— taxes, trade, labor—and did not evoke the same fear of special industry orientation.

Time Deadlines on Interagency Review

The Ash report devotes considerable space to the problem of delays in agency proceedings that result from slow review by commissioners of staff decisions. Some regulatory commissions insist on reviewing all decisions by hearing examiners; other agencies that have devised rules to permit some types of hearing examiner decisions to become final without review have, nevertheless, ended up reviewing an enormously large fraction of all decisions. Most of the experts at the conference agreed that streamlining agency decision-making through more limited internal review procedures was desirable. Yet no one supported the proposal that commissions or agency administrators be given only thirty days to decide to review a case. In the words of one discussant, "The review period is so short that it suggests a summary, preemptory type of review. What this may well mean is a drastic shift of the review function from the agency to the court, which could be rather counterproductive to the Ash Council's own purposes."

Several conferees believe that there are other mechanisms for expediting internal review, some of which are already in operation in some agencies. Some cited the Federal Communications Commission Review Board as an example of a mechanism for freeing commissioners from the task of reviewing all cases within the agency. Another suggested that the hearing examiner's hand could be strengthened if regulatory commissions were required to make specific policy statements each time they decided not to accept the recommendation of the hearing examiner. To review a decision, a commission would have to be willing to write clarifying policy; in overturning a decision, the hearing examiner would be presented with a clear guideline for future cases.

The proposal to experiment with a time limit on intra-agency review commanded considerable support. Agencies should not be permitted to make policy in a negative fashion by interminably delaying procedures. But 30 days was thought to be an absurdly short period; 90 and 120 days were mentioned as more reasonable.

Combining Transportation Agencies

The proposal to merge the three transportation agencies—the Interstate Commerce Commission (ICC), the Civil Aeronautics Board (CAB), and the Federal Maritime Commission (FMC)—was recognized as having some potential advantages. Obviously, a single transportation agency would have more opportunity to make a rational transportation policy, since the information and motivation for coordinated planning would reside in a single decision-making body. One conferee also suggested that bringing all transportation regulation into a single agency might eliminate some of the industry orientation of the regulators. The merger would focus attention on regulatory issues more general than the problems of a single mode and would give transport regulators a broader constituency, which would permit individual decisions against particular interests.

Nevertheless, several conferees were skeptical about the proposal. The most important criticism was that consolidation would eliminate the last vestige of competition in transportation—an industry that should probably not even be regulated (in terms of prices and entry) in the first place. In the words of one discussant, consolidation "runs the risk of creating the opportunity to enforce unwise policies even more effectively and to run a better cartel, thereby eliminating the intermodal competition now thought to be the one saving grace." Others argued that agencies with multiple responsibilities tend to adopt a single industry or regulatory function as the central focus of the agency: textile and fur labeling in the Federal Trade Commission (FTC), broadcasting in the Federal Communications Commission (FCC), and motor carriers in the ICC. Since the dominant force in a merged transportation agency would probably be the ICC, consolidation might simply provide a mechanism for regulating airlines and international shipping in the interest of trucks.

While recognizing these dangers, a few conferees still concluded that a merger of the transportation agencies should be tried, if for no other reason than that it might shake up transportation regulation. One conferee taking this position argued as follows:

Nearly all of the mischief that consolidation can accomplish has already been done by consolidating all of domestic surface transportation regulation in the ICC. The transportation regulated by the ICC is not a close enough competitor with airlines or international water carriers to be worth worrying about. I am more concerned about undoing the mischief already done than about the 10 percent more mischief that potentially could be done after consolidation.

Breaking up the FTC

The proposal to split the Federal Trade Commission into two new agencies, one dealing with consumer protection and the other with antitrust activity, met with strong disapproval at the conference. Two arguments were made for keeping the two activities together. First, they are really one function—protecting consumers against business abuses, either noncompetitive pricing or product misrepresentation. Second, the consumer protection responsibilities give the FTC a strong proconsumer constituency, which carries over into its antitrust activity. The renaissance of the FTC in the last two years, which spread through all functions of the agency, was seen as a result of the emergence of consumer groups as an important political force. Finally, one conferee argued that it was particularly inappropriate to break up, and implicitly punish for its behavior, the one regulatory agency that seems to be coming out of a long period of inactivity and taking command of its regulatory responsibilities.

Several conferees suggested that, rather than to break up the FTC, a better action would be to consolidate the FTC and the Antitrust division of the Department of Justice into a single independent agency. The principal argument in favor of this proposal was that the coordination of antitrust policy would be facilitated. In the case of merger policy, for example, the two agencies have taken somewhat inconsistent positions. The disadvantages of the proposal were (1) the concentration of power in one body or, in the case of a single administrator, one man; and (2) the difficulty of melding the differences in powers and approach of the two agencies. The FTC, a court-like body, has subpoena power and other tools not available to the Antitrust division, while the latter is more prosecutor than judge. Many conferees believed that, because of the political visibility of the attorney general, folding the FTC's powers into the Antitrust division probably would not be as wise as merging the latter into the former and retaining independent status for the consolidated agency.

Alternatives to the Ash Proposals

Nearly all of the conferees believed that the principal objectives of regulatory reform should be the deregulation of certain markets in which competition appears to be both feasible and beneficial, and more effective regulation elsewhere—particularly in the fields of monopoly pricing and consumer protection. Since the conferees unanimously agreed that organizational changes were unlikely to provide help to regulatory agencies in accomplishing either objective, the conference focused on a number of more substantial, but controversial, alternative proposals.

Economists in Regulatory Positions

One group favored appointing economists to regulatory commissions and even to the courts responsible for reviewing regulatory decisions. (This view *was not* held by all economists present at the meeting, and *was* held by a few noneconomists!) The principal argument supporting this proposal was that regulation is essentially an aspect of economic policy. To pursue economic policy effectively and in the public interest requires technical economic expertise. One discussant characterized the case for more economists in decision-making roles in the following way:

The process of infusing economic knowledge into litigation now requires filtering economic arguments through lawyers. In regulatory commissions the filter is very imperfect. What comes through are the answers an economist can provide to a regulatory problem, but not the process used to produce those answers. The commissioners understand the answers, but not the logical argument behind them. For example, this is essentially the case in rate-base, rate-of-return regulation. I can tell you that the proper rate of return is 7.5263 percent; two other economists can give two different numbers. A common procedure is for a commission to take the average of the three numbers, rather than to try to assess the arguments supporting each estimate, because the supporting arguments are incomprehensible to noneconomists. We are at the stage where capital market theory is so complex that people can make a lot of money on it, and those who know it better make more money. Economists are for sale, and in a competitive market you can find an economist who will say almost anything. You have to know why they are saying what they say and the reasoning behind it. When we are at that stage, a commissioner cannot be his own economist: he cannot do it for free any more.

Obviously, economists in regulatory agencies or on courts are likely to judge the wisdom of a regulatory action primarily by economic criteria. The conferees were divided on the proposal to have more economists in regulation, according to whether they believed economic issues should be paramount in regulatory policy. For example, if the object of the price structure in commercial air service is to maximize the number of planes flown and cities served, economists would probably prove counterproductive to the regulatory process. On the other hand, if the purpose of regulation is to insure that air travel is provided where economically justified and to keep prices reasonably in line with costs, economists could play a central role in formulating and enforcing regulatory policy.

Deregulation

Another group concluded that effective regulation—particularly of prices and entry—was probably impossible and proposed that much regulation ought to be dispensed with. Most popular was the proposal to deregulate transportation, particularly surface transportation. A somewhat smaller group believed that power and communications also should be deregulated. The proponents of deregulation would retain consumer protection and antitrust activities. The latter would be relied on to control monopolistic practices of regulated public utilities, which are now to a significant degree exempt from antitrust prosecution.

The proponents of deregulation did not claim that, in principle, price regulation of monopolies was a bad idea on ideological grounds. Rather, their case was based on the observation that regulation is expensive, ineffective, and even anticompetitive. Having seen regulatory agencies of all types and organizational forms become oriented toward protecting the regulated industry, proponents of deregulation conclude that effective regulation is probably impossible, except perhaps when the agency is cast in the role of an advocate of one side of a dispute between the general public and a particular industry or firm, or in the rare instance when the interests of the general public and the industry are largely coincident (as in much of securities or aircraft safety regulation).

Nationalization

A final group suggested that only through nationalization could society have any hope of effectively controlling the behavior of monopolistic industries. Most of the conferees on both sides of the nationalization issue recognized that their views on the matter were largely instinctive. Little evidence has been gathered to support the case for or against government ownership of public utilities, concentrated industries, or industries in which an enormous amount of national welfare is tied up (such as drugs). The only serious call for substantially more research made during the conference was with respect to nationalization. Several conferees on both sides of the nationalization debate believed that economists should undertake in-depth comparative studies of policies in other nations toward industries that are regulated in the United States but unregulated or nationalized elsewhere.

Some proponents of nationalization believed that a good first step toward nationalizing public utilities would be to deregulate them first. The probable results of deregulation, they believed, would be: (1) no substantial change in prices, (2) a significant redistribution of services offered in different areas, and (3) an enormous increase in the profits of the industries. The high profits would make clear the need for government action to bring prices more in line with costs, but the historical failure of regulation to accomplish this end—a failure made obvious by the results of deregulation—would lead to public demand for nationalization.

Conclusions

The Brookings conference of experts left one overriding impression: Most of the experts present believed that much of regulation in the United States is in deep trouble. As is obvious from the roster of conference participants, the conference was not designed to represent a particular view. Former commissioners appointed during both Republican and Democratic administrations, academic experts from three disciplines, and individuals who had held high staff positions in regulatory agencies in both the 1950s and the 1960s, while often differing in their assessment of the causes and possible cures of regulatory failures, nevertheless recognized the critical state of affairs in regulation. Furthermore, nearly all conferees agreed that the essence of the problem is that regulators, for whatever reason, consider too narrow a range of issues, information, and interests in making decisions, whether on matters of policy or on specific cases. Finally, a substantial majority of the participants were of the opinion that the primary purpose of regulation should be to contribute to economic efficiency—promoting competition, keeping prices in line with costs, permitting cost-reducing or service-augmenting technological change, and perfecting consumer knowledge of product quality. The objectives that appear paramount in much of regulation at present—to reduce, if not eliminate, producer uncertainty and to preserve uneconomic services—were held to be at best of considerably lower priority and, more likely, inappropriate.

Most conferees also believed that a blanket condemnation of all regulation and a concomitant proposal to reform every regulatory agency are not justified. Many gave relatively high marks to the recent activities of the Federal Trade Commission, for example. The apparent lack of a correlation between organizational structure and performance was held to be a valid criticism of the Ash report.

Commanding support was the view that agencies benefit from occasionally being shaken up. Many conferees argued that the strong, persistent criticism of regulation during the past fifteen years has had a profound impact on the quality of regulation. Regulation works better if its quality is an important public issue. The scandals of the 1950s, the attacks by outgoing commissioners throughout the 1960s, the criticism of consumer champions like Ralph Nader, and the results of recent scholarly research have all served to increase the public pressure on regulatory agencies. One conference participant, who was not contradicted by the others, suggested that because of greater political visibility regulation may well be more beneficial to the general public today than ever before.

The above account of what is happening in regulation is not a defense of the proposition that regulation is now performing well; however, it has a rather optimistic tone. It does suggest that the regulatory process just might be made to function better if the constituency of the regulatory agencies could be broadened. Thus, proposals to give public interest groups public financial support and legal standing before regulatory agencies might prove effective.

Some conferees were less optimistic, believing that only the extremes of deregulation or nationalization hold significant hope for improving the performance of many regulated sectors. But the pessimists were in the minority. The majority were optimistic that reform of regulation was possible, and in this regard they shared the view of the Ash Council. Yet even the optimistic majority believed that far more than the organizational structure of regulation needs reforming. Reorganization—at least after the temporary effects of a shakeup wear off—does not change fundamentally the environment in which regulatory policy is made: the legal, political, and procedural setting, the expertise of the decision makers, the legislative mandate. According to the experts, if regulation is to be made significantly more effective, profound changes must be made in some of these components of the regulatory environment.

The Findings and Recommendations
of the Ash Council

The following are the findings of the President's Advisory Council on Executive Organization (the Ash Council) concerning regulatory agencies, and the Council's recommendations for reform. They are quoted from A New Regulatory Framework: Report on Selected Independent Regulatory Agencies *(1971), pages 3-7.*

Major and fundamental change pervades each of the areas of economic enterprise under regulation by the independent regulatory commissions.

In transportation, increasing interaction between the various modes reflects a persistent striving for greater efficiency in the movement of goods and people;

In trade, new and probably enduring levels of public and producer attention are being given to the quality of goods and services, and to the operation of the marketplace;

In securities, even as the structure of the industry itself and the relationship between government and industry are experiencing major changes, a well-established trend toward institutional investment and new methods of financing are significantly altering the characteristics of securities trading;

In power, where industry structure is also undergoing change, supplies of electrical energy and natural gas have not consistently kept pace with increasing demands in certain areas, and new technologies have yet to take up the slack;

In communications, burgeoning technology has created new avenues for service and new products which together complicate the task of regulation and blur distinctions between the various forms of communications.

The independent regulatory commissions play a critical role in balancing the changing demands of the nation for the goods and services of regulated industries and the related need for financially sound and effectively managed industries in the regulated sectors of our economy. Unfortunately, obsolete organizational forms limit the effectiveness of these commissions in responding to economic, technological, structural, and social change. Inappropriate regulatory structures and cumbersome procedures impose burdens that impede good public service, sound financial and operational planning, and adjustment to changes in growing industries—contrary to the purposes of regulation.

Our proposals for change in the organizational forms of several independent regulatory commissions are directed at improving agency effectiveness, while assuring fairness to those involved in or affected by the regulatory process.

Findings

The regulatory commissions are not sufficiently accountable for their actions to either the Congress or the President because of the degree of their independence and remoteness in practice from those constitutional branches of government. Regulatory activities, therefore, are not adequately supported and are not effectively coordinated with national policy goals.

Inherent deficiencies in the commission form of organization prevent the commissions from responding effectively to changes in industry structure, technology, economic trends, and public needs.

Deficiencies in the performance of the regulatory commissions are partly due to the difficulty of attracting highly qualified commissioners and retaining executive staff. Even able administrators have difficulty in serving as coequals on collegial commissions.

While there are notable exceptions, it is difficult to attract to regulatory positions men of skill in administration and breadth of perspective largely because of the procedures and traditions associated with appointment to the regulatory commissions.

Given these traditions and the shared responsibility of the collegial form, it is not likely that commission positions will generate greater interest in the future.

Certain judicial activities of the commissions conflict with their policy-making responsibilities and generate an organizational environment inimical to regulatory efficiency and constructive response to industry and the public.

Many commissions engage excessively in case-by-case adjudication as a basis for policy formulation rather than using less formal procedures such as exchanges of written or oral information, informal regulatory guidance, or rulemaking.

The judicial cast of agency review proceedings places too great an emphasis on legal perspectives to the detriment of economic, financial, technical, and social perspectives. One result is a high level of legal skill among agency professionals and commissioners, but generally insufficient capability in other disciplines.

The judicial cast of agency review proceedings delays final administrative determinations and invites dilatory appeals.

Overjudicialization encumbers the time and energies of commissioners and staff, causes undue case backlogs, imposes high costs upon litigants, prevents anticipatory action through rulemaking, deters informal settlements, and precludes coordination of agency policy and priorities with those of the executive branch.

Certain functional responsibilities are inappropriately distributed among the various commissions.

Responsibility for regulation of transportation is distributed among the ICC, CAB, and FMC, impeding formulation of broader regulatory policy covering the several transportation modes and coordination with the Department of Transportation, and thus forestalling consistency in national transportation policy.

Responsibility for promotion of transportation, vested in some regulatory commissions, conflicts with the regulatory activity of those agencies.

Combination of antitrust enforcement and consumer protection in the FTC deprives that agency of a central purpose, fostering an uncertainty of emphasis as between its functions, inordinate delay, and preoccupation with routine matters.

Regulation of public utility holding companies by the SEC is no longer best performed by that agency. Regulatory expertise regarding public utility holding companies rests with the FPC.

Recommendations

To assure coordination of regulatory matters with national policy goals, to improve the management efficiency of regulatory functions, to improve accountability to the Congress and the executive branch and to increase the probability of superior leadership for regulatory activities, the transportation, power, securities, and consumer protection regulatory functions should be administered by single administrators, appointed by the President. These functions should be performed by agencies respectively designated: Transportation Regulatory Agency, Federal Power Agency, Securities and Exchange Agency, and Federal Trade Practices Agency.

The authority and responsibility attending the single administrator form should enable the agencies to attract and retain the most highly qualified administrators and executive staffs.

Unambiguous placement of authority for agency policy and operations in a single administrator should increase accountability to both the Congress and the President.

Agency work should be expedited by utilizing more effective administrative techniques made possible by one-man management of agency activities.

The communications regulatory function and the antitrust enforcement function should, as now, be carried out by multimember bodies for reasons supervening the advantages of a single administrator. The FCC should be reduced in size from seven to five members, to serve 5-year terms.

To prevent the overjudicialization of agency procedures and attitudes and to assure comprehensive and anticipatory policymaking, internal agency review of proceedings should be limited in time and focused primarily on the consistency of the decision with agency policy. Appeals from final agency decisions should be heard by an Administrative Court of the United States.

A 30-day period should be allowed after a hearing examiner's decision for review by the single administrator. The administrator should have the power to modify or remand an examiner's decisions. The limited time and scope of policy review by agency administrators should help make initial decisions of agency examiners, in many cases, final determinations of the agency.

The Administrative Court should review appeals by an aggrieved party from final agency determinations of the transportation, securities and power agencies. Decisions of the antitrust, trade practices, and communications agencies would be reviewed in the federal courts as they are today.

The court should consist of as many as 15 judges, appointed by the President and confirmed by the Senate for terms sufficiently long as to attract men of quality. We suggest 15-year staggered terms, with judges sitting in three-man panels for each case reviewed by the court.

Certain functional responsibilities of the agencies should be realigned.

To reflect the increasing interdependence of the structure, economics, and technology of the transportation modes, regulatory responsibilities of the ICC, CAB, and the FMC should be combined within a new Transportation Regulatory Agency.

To correct the conflict inherent in performing regulatory and promotional functions in the same agency, the promotional subsidy-granting activities of the CAB should be transferred to the Department of Transportation.

To assure that each of its missions is more effectively performed, the FTC's consumer protection responsibilities should be vested in a new Federal Trade Practices Agency and its antitrust enforcement responsibilities should be vested in a new Federal Antitrust Board. The Board should consist of a chairman and two economist members, each appointed by the President with the consent of the Senate.

To provide an organizational placement which better reflects current realities, the regulatory responsibilities of the SEC under the Public Utility Holding Company Act should be transferred to the Federal Power Agency.

Brookings Conference Participants

Alexander M. Bickel *Yale Law School*
James Bonnen *Michigan State University*
Stephen Breyer *Harvard University*
Clark M. Byse *Harvard University*
Kenneth A. Cox *Microwave Communications, Inc.*
Roger C. Cramton *Administrative Conference of the United States*
Lloyd N. Cutler *Wilmer, Cutler & Pickering*
Kenneth C. Davis *University of Chicago*
John A. Ferejohn *Brookings Institution*[1]
Frederick W. Ford *Pittman, Lovett, Ford, Hennessey and White*
Kermit Gordon *Brookings Institution*
Edwin T. Haefele *Resources for the Future*
Charles Haywood *University of Kentucky*
Louis J. Hector *Scott, McCarthy, Steel, Hector, and Davis*
Phillip S. Hughes *Brookings Institution*
Gerald R. Jantscher *Brookings Institution*
Herbert Kaufman *Brookings Institution*
Lawrence B. Krause *Brookings Institution*
Samuel Krislov *University of Minnesota*
Paul W. MacAvoy *Massachusetts Institute of Technology*
James W. McKie *Brookings Institution*[2]
Willard F. Mueller *University of Wisconsin*
Roger G. Noll *Brookings Institution*
Mark Novitch *Department of Health, Education, and Welfare*
Joseph A. Pechman *Brookings Institution*
Merton J. Peck *Yale University*
Lewis A. Rivlin *Peabody, Rivlin, Kelly, Cladouhos and Lambert*
Glen O. Robinson *University of Minnesota*
Richard A. Solomon *Wilner, Scheiner, & Greeley*
Lee C. White *Semer, White and Jacobsen*
Edwin M. Zimmerman *Covington and Burling*

1. Mr. Ferejohn is now at the California Institute of Technology.
2. Mr. McKie is now at the University of Texas.